Public and Private Morality

Public and Private Morality

EDITED BY

STUART HAMPSHIRE
Warden of Wadham College, Oxford

CAMBRIDGE UNIVERSITY PRESS
Cambridge
London   New York   New Rochelle
Melbourne   Sydney

Published by the Press Syndicate of the University of Cambridge
The Pitt Building, Trumpington Street, Cambridge CB2 1RP
32 East 57th Street, New York, NY 10022, USA
296 Beaconsfield Parade, Middle Park, Melbourne 3206, Australia

First published 1978
Reprinted 1979

Printed in Great Britain at the
University Press, Cambridge

Library of Congress Cataloguing in Publication Data

Main entry under title:

Public and private morality.

CONTENTS: Hampshire, S. Morality and pessimism. –
Hampshire, S. Public and private morality. –
Williams, B. Politics and moral character. [etc.]

1. Political ethics – Addresses, essays, lectures.
I. Hampshire, Stuart, 1914–
JA79.P8   172   78–2839
ISBN 0 521 22084 X hard covers
ISBN 0 521 29352 9 paperback

Contents

Contributors

RONALD DWORKIN, *Professor of Jurisprudence in the University of Oxford*

STUART HAMPSHIRE, *Warden of Wadham College, Oxford*

THOMAS NAGEL, *Department of Philosophy, Princeton University, Princeton, N.J.*

T. M. SCANLON, *Department of Philosophy, Princeton University, Princeton, N.J.*

BERNARD WILLIAMS, *Knightbridge Professor of Moral Philosophy in the University of Cambridge*

Foreword

'Ceux qui voudront traiter séparément la politique et la morale n'entendront jamais rien à aucune de deux.' So Rousseau in *Émile*, and it is a judgment in the classical Greek tradition which I accept. This book had its origins in the thought of one question in the vast, continuous subject of morals-and-politics: the question unforgettably displayed by Machiavelli for every subsequent generation to consider. His was the problem of political realism: what is the relation, and what ought to be the relation, between political violence and political deceit on the one side and, on the other, the minimum acceptable moral standards which define human decency and which encourage or permit a tolerable quality of social life? What are the limits to be set upon grossly immoral and cruel practices which sometimes also effectively protect and promote great public causes? These questions are always pressing and difficult to answer and they were re-formulated in many of the arguments circling around the Vietnam War. Hearing some of the principal defenders of American policy at the time, and reading some of the documents, one had the clear impression that a simplified Machiavellianism, a naive contempt for 'moralistic' attitudes, had in recent years become influential among policy-makers in the U.S.A. and elsewhere. The problem of how to think consistently and responsibly about the horrors of violence and of cruelty, also of deceit, which are often incidental to policy-making, has not been much explored recently by moral philosophers. Although the dividing line between private life and public responsibilities can never be definite and clear, there is a moral threshold which is crossed both by those who assume power to change the lives of many men through public action and by those who undertake to represent in a public role the will and interests of many other men. A new responsibility, and even a new kind of responsibility, and new moral conflicts, present themselves.

Of the six essays in this book three directly confront Machia-velli's problem, which is a single complex question in political philosophy: Professor Nagel's 'Ruthlessness in Public Life' and my essay 'Public and Private Morality' and Professor Bernard Williams' 'Politics and Moral Character'. Each of us approaches the question from his own moral point of view, and with theoretical considerations in mind, and we would not claim to have examined every facet of the problem. The papers by Professor Scanlon and Professor Dworkin traverse rather broader issues of political theory, singling out and characterising the type of moral claim upon which political arguments turn. In both these essays the notion of rights is at the centre of the argument and in both cases the argument looks for the rational foundation of contemporary liberal attitudes. 'Morality and Pessimism' originated as a Leslie Stephen Lecture delivered in the University of Cambridge on 24 February 1972, with the relation between public policy and moral restraints as one of its themes.

1　Morality and Pessimism

STUART HAMPSHIRE

I shall examine a current of moral ideas which was partly philosophical and partly something less precise, a movement in public consciousness. British utilitarianism was a school of moral thought, and a school also of general philosophy, which set out to do good in the world, even though it was only a philosophy; and it may even be judged to have succeeded in large part over many years in this aim. It is certainly not easy, and perhaps it is not possible, to calculate the real effect upon men's lives of any new system of moral ideas and of any new philosophy. But the utilitarian philosophy brought new interests into the study of political economy: into the theory and practice of public administration: into the rhetoric, and into the programmes, of movements of political and social reform in Britain. Indeed the utilitarian philosophy became part of the ordinary furniture of the minds of those enlightened persons, who would criticise institutions, not from the standpoint of one of the Christian churches, but from a secular point of view. As represented by Sidgwick at Cambridge, and in the minds of liberal and radical social reformers everywhere, the utilitarian philosophy was until quite recently a constant support for progressive social policies. Even the rare and strange adaptation of utilitarianism, which appeared in the last chapter of G. E. Moore's *Principia Ethica*, pointed towards liberal and improving policies: at least it did in the minds of Keynes, of Leonard Woolf and of others whose lives were seriously influenced by Moore. Moore himself wrote of his own moral conclusions as prescribing the aims of social policy, and, like Mill, he was marking the target of social improvements. The utilitarian philosophy, before the First World War and for many years after it – perhaps even until 1939 – was still a bold, innovative, even a subversive doctrine, with a record of successful social criticism behind it. I believe that it is losing this role, and that it is now an obstruction.

Utilitarianism has always been a comparatively clear moral theory, with a simple core and central notion, easily grasped and easily translated into practical terms. Its essential instruction goes like this: when assessing the value of institutions, habits, conventions, manners, rules, and laws, and also when considering the merits of individual actions or policies, turn your attention to the actual or probable states of mind of the persons who are, or will be, affected by them: that is all you need to consider in your assessments. In a final analysis, nothing else counts but the states of mind, and perhaps, more narrowly, the states of feeling, of persons; or, more generously in Bentham and G. E. Moore, of sentient creatures. Anything else that one might consider, in the indefinite range of natural and man-made things, is to be reckoned as mere machinery, as only a possible instrument for producing the all-important – literally all-important – states of feeling. From this moral standpoint, the whole machinery of the natural order, other than states of mind, just is machinery, useful or harmful in proportion as it promotes or prevents desired states of feeling.

For a utilitarian, the moral standpoint, which is to govern all our actions, places men at the very centre of the universe, with their states of feeling as the source of all value in the world. If the species perished, to the last man, or if the last men became impassible and devoid of feeling, things would become cold and indifferent and neutral, from the moral point of view; whether this or that other unfeeling species survived or perished, plants, stars, and galaxies, would then be of no consequence. Destruction of things is evil only in so far as it is, or will be, felt as a loss by sentient beings; and the creation of things, and the preservation of species, are to be aimed at and commended only in so far as sentient beings are, or will be, emotionally and sentimentally interested in the things created and preserved.

This doctrine may reasonably be criticised in two contrary ways: first, as involving a kind of arrogance in the face of nature, an arrogance that is intelligible only if the doctrine is seen as a residue of the Christian account of our species' peculiar relation to the Creator. Without the Christian story it seems to entail a strangely arbitrary narrowing of moral interest. Is the destruction, for instance, of a species in nature to be avoided, as a great evil, only or principally because of the loss of the pleasure that human beings may derive from the species? May the natural order be farmed by human beings for their comfort and pleasure without any restriction other than the comfort and pleasure of future human beings? Perhaps there is no rational procedure for answering these questions. But it is strange to answer them with a confident 'Yes'. On the other hand the doctrine that only our feelings are morally significant may be thought, on the contrary, to belittle men: for it makes morality, the system of rights, duties and obligations, a kind of psychical engineering, which shows the way to induce desired or valued states of mind. This suggests, as a corollary, that men might be trained, moulded, even bred, with a view to their experiencing the kinds of feeling that alone lend value to their morally neutral surroundings. With advancing knowledge states of the soul might be controlled by chemical means, and the valuable experiences of the inner life may be best prolonged and protected by a medical technique. So the original sense of the sovereign importance of human beings, and of their feelings, has been converted by exaggeration into its opposite: a sense that these original ends of action are, or may soon become, comparatively manageable problems in applied science.

From the standpoint of philosophy, in a full, old-fashioned sense of that word, we have moved, slowly, stage by stage, in the years since 1914, into a different world of thought from that which most of Leslie Stephen's contemporaries inhabited; and by a 'world of thought' here I mean the set of conditioning assumptions which any European, who thought in a philosophical way about morality, would have in mind before he started to think, assumptions that he probably would not examine one by one, and that he would with difficulty make explicit to himself. One such assumption was that, even if the transcendental claims of Christianity have been denied, any serious thought about morality must acknowledge the absolute exceptionalness of men, the unique dignity and worth of this species among otherwise speechless, inattentive things, and their uniquely open future; how otherwise can morality have its overriding claims? A second assumption, explicit in J. S. Mill, and unchallenged by his utilitarian successors, was that both emotional sensitiveness, and intelligence in the calculation of consequences, can be expected to multiply and increase, as moral enlightenment spreads and as standards of education improve, into an indefinite and open future. In this open future there will be less avoidable waste of human happiness, less unconsidered destruction of positive and valued feelings, as the human sciences develop and superstitions become weaker and softer. The story of the past – this is the assumption – is essentially the story of moral waste, of a lack of clear planning and contrivance, of always repeated losses of happiness because no one methodically added the emotional gains and losses, with a clear head and undistracted by moral prejudices. The modern utilitarian policy-makers will be careful social economists, and their planning mistakes will be progressively corrigible ones; so there is no reason why there should not be a steadily rising balance of positive over negative feelings in all societies that have a rational computational morality. A new era of development is possible, the equivalent in morality of high technology in production.

This implicit optimism has been lost, not so much because of philosophical arguments but perhaps rather because of the hideous face of political events. Persecutions, massacres, and wars have been coolly justified by calculations of the long range benefit to mankind; and political pragmatists, in the advanced countries, using cost–benefit analyses prepared for them by gifted professors, continue to burn and destroy. The utilitarian habit of mind has brought with it a new abstract cruelty in politics, a dull, destructive political righteousness: mechanical, quantitative thinking, leaden academic minds setting out their moral calculations in leaden abstract prose, and more civilised and more superstitious people destroyed because of enlightened calculations that have proved wrong. Suppose a typical situation of political decision, typical, that is, of the present, and likely to be typical of the immediate future; an expert adviser has to present a set of possible policies between which a final choice has to be made; advantages and disadvantages of various outcomes are to be calculated, and a balance is to be struck. The methods of calculation may be quite sophisticated, and very disparate items may appear in the columns of gain and loss. The death of groups of persons may, for example, be balanced as a loss against a very considerable gain in amenity to be handed down to posterity; or a loss of liberty among one group may be balanced against a very great relief from poverty for another. Such calculations are the every day stuff of political decision, and they seem to require a common measure that enables qualitatively unrelated effects to be held in balance. The need to calculate in this manner, and to do so convincingly, plainly becomes greater as the area of government decision is widened, and as the applied social sciences render remote effects more computable.

Given that the vast new powers of government are in any case going to be used, and given that remote and collateral effects of policies are no longer utterly incalculable, and therefore to be neglected, a common measure to strike a balance is certain to be asked for and to be used; and apparently incommensurable interests will be brought together under this common measure. The utilitarian doctrine, insisting that there is a common measure of those gains and losses, which superficially seem incommensurable, is in any case called into being by the new conditions of political calculation. Any of the original defects in the doctrine will now be blown up, as a photograph is blown up, and made clearly visible in action.

For Machiavelli and his contemporaries, a political calculation was still a fairly simple computation of intended consequences, not unlike the stratagems of private intrigue. He and his contemporaries had no thought that a political calculation might issue in a plan for the future of a whole society or nation, with all kinds of dissimilar side-effects allowed for, and fed into the computation. Computation by a common measure now seems the most orthodox way to think in politics, although this kind of computation had originally been almost scandalous. At first the scandal and surprise lingered around the notion that moral requirements, and moral outrages, could be represented as commensurable gains and losses along a single scale. Yet now those who talk about being responsible in political decision believe that the moral issues must be represented on a common scale, if they are to be counted at all. How can the future of an advanced society be reasonably discussed and planned, if not on this assumption? To others, and particularly to many of the young in America and in Europe, who would not quote Burke, it seems now obvious that the large-scale computations in modern politics and social planning bring with them a coarseness and grossness of moral feeling, a blunting of sensibility, and a suppression of individual discrimination and gentleness, which are a price that they will not pay for the benefits of clear calculation. Their point is worth considering: perhaps it can be given a philosophical basis.

Allow me to go back to the beginnings of moral theory: as a non-commital starting-point, it may be agreed that we all assess ourselves, and other people, as having behaved well or badly, on a particular occasion, or for a tract of time, or taking a life-time as a whole. We similarly assess courses of action, and even whole ways of life, that are open to us before we make a decision. The more fundamental and overriding assessments, in relation to which all other assessments of persons are subsidiary and conditional, we call moral assessments, just because we count them as unconditional and overriding. The goodness or badness imputed may be imputed as a characteristic of persons, or of their actions, their decisions and their policies, or of their character and their dispositions, or of their lives and ways of life. Let me take the assessment of persons as the starting-point. When we assess ourselves or others in some limited role or capacity, as performing well or ill in that role or capacity, the assessment is not fundamental and unconditional; the assessment gives guidance only to someone who wants to have that role or to act in that capacity, or who wants to make use of someone who does. But if we assess persons as good or bad without further qualification or limitation, merely as human beings, and similarly also their decisions, policies, characters, dispositions, ways of life, as being good or bad without qualification, then our assessments have unconditional implications in respect of what should and should not be done, and of what people should, and should not be like, of their character, dispositions and way of life. A human being has the power to reflect on what kind of person he wants to be, and to try to act accordingly, within the limits of his circumstances. His more considered practical choices, and the conflicts that accompany them, will show what he holds to be intrinsically worth pursuing, and will therefore reveal his fundamental moral beliefs.

I believe that all I have so far said about this starting-point of moral philosophy is non-committal between different theories, and is innocent and unquestion-begging, and will be, or ought to be, accepted by moral philosophers of quite different persuasions, including the utilitarians. I believe this, because the various classical moral philosophies can all be formulated within this non-committal framework. Each moral philosophy singles out some ultimate ground or grounds for unconditional praise of persons, and prescribes the ultimate grounds for preferring one way of life to another. This is no less true of a utilitarian ethics than of any other; the effectively beneficent and happy man is accounted by a utilitarian more praiseworthy and admirable than any other type of man, and his useful life is thought the best kind of life that anyone could have, merely in virtue of its usefulness, and apart from any other characteristics it may have. The utilitarian philosophy picks out its own essential virtues very clearly, and the duties of a utilitarian are not hard to discern, even though they may on occasion involve difficult computations.

But there is one feature of familiar moralities which utilitarian ethics famously repudiates, or at least makes little of. There are a number of different moral prohibitions, apparent barriers to action, which a man acknowledges and which he thinks of as more or less insurmountable, except in abnormal, painful and improbable circumstances. One expects to meet these prohibitions, barriers to action, in certain quite distinct and clearly marked areas of action; these are the taking of human life, sexual relations, family duties and obligations, and the administration of justice according to the laws and customs of a given society. There are other areas in which strong barriers are to be expected; but these are, I think, the central and obvious ones. A morality is, at the very least, the regulation of the taking of life and the regulation of sexual relations, and it also includes rules of distributive and corrective justice: family duties: almost always duties of friendship: also rights and duties in respect of money and property. When specific prohibitions in these areas are probed and challenged by reflection, and the rational grounds for them looked for, the questioner will think that he is questioning a particular morality specified by particular prohibitions. But if he were to question the validity of recognising any prohibitions in these areas, he would think of himself as challenging the claims of morality itself; for the notion of morality requires that there be some strong barriers against the taking of life, against some varieties of sexual and family relations, against some forms of trial and punishment, some taking of property, and against some distributions of rewards and benefits.

Moral theories of the philosophical kind are differentiated in part by the different accounts that they give of these prohibitions: whether the prohibitions are to be thought of as systematically connected or not: whether they are absolute prohibitions or to be thought of as conditional. Utilitarians always had, and still have, very definite answers: first, they *are* systematically connected, and, secondly, they are to be thought of as not absolute, but conditional, being dependent for their validity as prohibitions upon the beneficial consequences of observing them. Plainly there is no possibility of proof here, since this is a question in ethics, and not in logic or in the experimental sciences. But various reasons for rejecting the utilitarian position can be given.

All of us sometimes speak of things that cannot be done, or that must be done, and that are ruled out as impossible by the nature of the case: also there are things that one must do, that one cannot not do, because of the nature of the case. The signs of necessity in such contexts mark the unqualified, unweakened, barrier to action, while the word 'ought', too much discussed in philosophical writing, conveys a weakened prohibition or instruction. The same contrast appears in the context of empirical statements, as in the judgments 'The inflation ought to stop soon' and 'The inflation must stop soon'. The modal words 'must' and 'ought' preserve a constant relation in a number of different types of discourse, of which moral argument is only one, not particularly conspicuous, example: he who in a shop says to the salesman 'The coat must cover my knees', alternatively, 'The coat ought to cover my knees', speaks of a need or requirement and of something less: he who, looking at the mathematical puzzle, says 'This must be the way to solve it', alternatively 'This ought to be the way to solve it', speaks of a kind of rational necessity, and of something less: examples of 'ought' as the weaker variant of 'must' could be indefinitely prolonged into other types of contexts. So 'He must help him' is the basic, unmodified judgment in the context of moral discussion or reflection, and 'He ought to help him' is its weakened variant, as it is in all other contexts. To learn what a man's moral beliefs are entails learning what he thinks that he must not do, at any cost or at almost any cost.

The range of the utterly forbidden types of conduct amongst Stephen's friends would differ significantly, but not greatly, from the range of the forbidden and the impossible that would be acknowledged in this room. Social anthropologists may record fairly wide variations in the range of the morally impossible, and also, I believe, some barriers that are very general, though not quite universal; and historians similarly. For example, in addition to certain fairly specific types of killing, certain fairly specific types of sexual promiscuity, certain takings of property, there are also types of disloyalty and of cowardice, particularly disloyalty to friends, which are very generally, almost universally, forbidden and forbidden absolutely: they are forbidden as being intrinsically disgraceful and unworthy, and as being, just for these reasons, ruled out: ruled out because they would be disgusting, or disgraceful, or shameful, or brutal, or inhuman, or base, or an outrage.

In arguing against utilitarians I must dwell a little on these epithets usually associated with morally impossible action, on a sense of disgrace, of outrage, of horror, of baseness, of brutality, and, most important, a sense that a barrier, assumed to be firm and almost insurmountable, has been knocked over, and a feeling that, if this horrible, or outrageous, or squalid, or brutal, action is possible, then anything is possible and nothing is forbidden, and all restraints are threatened. Evidently these ideas have often been associated with impiety, and with a belief that God, or the Gods, have been defied, and with a fear of divine anger. But they need not have these associations with the supernatural, and they may have, and often have had, a secular setting. In the face of the doing of something that must not be done, and that is categorically excluded and forbidden morally, the fear that one may feel is fear of human nature. A relapse into a state of nature seems a real possibility: or perhaps seems actually to have occurred, unless an alternative morality with new restraints is clearly implied when the old barrier is crossed. This fear of human nature, and sense of outrage, when a barrier is broken down, is an aspect of respect for morality itself rather than for any particular morality and for any particular set of prohibitions.

The notion of the morally impossible – 'I cannot leave him now: it would be quite impossible'. 'Surely you understand that I *must* help him' – is distinct. A course of conduct is ruled out ('You cannot do that'), because it would be inexcusably unjust, or dishonest, or humiliating, or treacherous, or cruel, or ungenerous, or harsh. These epithets, specifying why the conduct is impossible, mark the vices characteristically recognised in a particular morality. In other societies, at other places and times, other specific epithets might be more usually associated with outrage and morally impossible conduct; but the outrage or shock, and the recognition of impossibility, will be the same in cases where the type of conduct rejected, and the reasons for the rejection, are rather different.

The utilitarian will not deny these facts, but he will interpret them differently. Shock, he will say, is the primitive, pre-rational reaction; after rational reflection the strength of feeling associated with a prohibition can be, and ought to be, proportional to the estimated harm of the immediate and remote consequences; and he will find no more in the signs of necessity and impossibility than an emphasis on the moral rules which have proved to be necessary protections against evil effects. The signs of necessity are signs that there is a rule. But the rational justification of there being a rule is to be found in the full consequences of its observance, and not in non-rational reactions of horror, disgust, shame, and other emotional repugnances.

But I believe that critical reflection may leave the notion of absolutely forbidden, because absolutely repugnant, conduct untouched. There may in many cases be good reflective reasons why doing such things, assuming such a character, may be abhorrent, and excluded from the range of possible conduct; there may be reflective reasons, in the sense that one is able to say why the conduct is impossible as destroying the ideal of a way of life that one aspires to and respects, as being, for example, utterly unjust or cruel or treacherous or corruptly dishonest. To show that these vices are vices, and unconditionally to be avoided, would take one back to the criteria for the assessment of persons as persons, and therefore to the whole way of life that one aspires to as the best way of life. A reflective, critical scrutiny of moral claims is compatible, both logically and psychologically, with an overriding concern for a record of un-monstrous and respectworthy conduct, and of action that has never been mean or inhuman; and it may follow an assessment of the worth of persons which is not to be identified only with a computation of consequences and effects.

There is a model of rational reflection which depends upon a contrast between the primitive moral response of an uneducated man, and of an uneducated society, and the comparatively detached arguments of the sophisticated moralist, who discounts his intuitive responses as being prejudices inherited from an uncritical past. Conspicuous in the philosophical radicals, in John Stuart Mill, and in the Victorian free-thinkers generally, this model in turn depended upon the idea that primitive, pre-scientific men are usually governed by strict moral taboos, and that in future intellectually evolved, and scientifically trained, men will be emancipated from these bonds, and will start again with clear reasoning about consequences. The word 'taboo', so often used in these contexts, shows the assumption of moral progress from primitive beginnings, and suggests a rather naive contrast between older moralities and the open morality of the future; empirical calculation succeeds a priori prejudice, and the calculation of consequences is reason.

But reflection may discover a plurality of clear and definite moral injunctions; injunctions about the taking of life, about sexual relations, about the conduct of parents towards children and of children towards parents, about one's duties in times of war, about the conditions under which truth must be told and under which it may be concealed, about rights of property, about duties of friendship, and so on over the various aspects and phases of a normal span of life. Such injunctions need not be inferrable from a few basic principles, corresponding to the axioms of a theory. The pattern that they form can have a different type of unity. Taken together, a full set of such injunctions, prohibiting types of conduct in types of circumstance, describes in rough and indeterminate outline, an attainable and recognisable way of life, aspired to, respected and admired: or at least the minimum general features of a respectworthy way of life. And a way of life is not identified and characterised by one distinct purpose, such as the increase of general happiness, or even by a set of such distinct purposes. The connection between the injunctions, the connection upon which a reasonable man reflects, is to be found in the coherence of a single way of life, distinguished by the characteristic virtues and vices recognised within it.

A way of life is a complicated thing, marked out by many

details of style and manner, and also by particular activities and interests, which a group of people of similar dispositions in a similar social situation may share; so that the group may become an imitatable human type who transmit many of their habits and ideals to their descendants, provided that social change is not too rapid.

In rational reflection one may justify an intuitively accepted and unconditional prohibition, as a common, expected feature of a recognisable way of life which on other grounds one values and finds admirable: or as a necessary preliminary condition of this way of life. There are rather precise grounds in experience and in history for the reasonable man to expect that certain virtues, which he admires and values, can only be attained at the cost of certain others, and that the virtues typical of several different ways of life cannot be freely combined, as he might wish. Therefore a reasonable and reflective person will review the separate moral injunctions, which intuitively present themselves as having force and authority, as making a skeleton of an attainable, respectworthy and preferred way of life. He will reject those that seem likely in practice to conflict with others that seem more closely part of, or conditions of, the way of life that he values and admires, or that seem irrelevant to this way of life.

One must not exaggerate the degree of connectedness that can be claimed for the set of injunctions that constitute the skeleton of a man's morality. For example, it is a loose, empirical connection that reasonably associates certain sexual customs with the observation of certain family duties, and certain loyalties to the state or country with the recognition of certain duties in respect of property, and in time of war. The phrase 'way of life' is vague and is chosen for its vagueness. The unity of a single way of life, and the compatibility in practice of different habits and dispositions, are learnt from observation, direct experience and from psychology and history; we know that human nature naturally varies, and is deliberately variable, only within limits; and that not all theoretically compatible achievements and enjoyments are compatible in normal circumstances. A reasonable man may envisage a way of life, which excludes various kinds of conduct as impossible, without excluding a great variety of morally tolerable ways of life within this minimum framework. The moral prohibitions constitute a kind of grammar of conduct, showing the elements out of which any fully respectworthy conduct, as one conceives it, must be built.

The plurality of absolute prohibitions, and the looseness of their association with any one way of life, which stresses a certain set of virtues, is to be contrasted with the unity and simplicity of utilitarian ethics. One might interpret the contrast in this way: to the utilitarian it is certain that all reasonable purposes are parts of a single purpose in a creature known to be governed by the pleasure principle or by a variant of it. The anti-utilitarian replies: nothing is certain in the *theory* of morality: but, at a pre-theoretical level, some human virtues fit together as virtues to form a way of life aspired to, and some monstrous and brutal acts are certainly vicious in the sense that they undermine and corrupt this way of life; and we can explain why they are, and what makes them so, provided that we do not insist upon either precision or certainty or simplicity in the explanation.

The absolute moral prohibitions, which I am defending, are not to be identified with Kant's categorical moral injunctions; for they are not to be picked out by the logical feature of being universal in form. Nor are they prescriptions that must be affirmed, and that cannot be questioned or denied, just because they are principles of rationality, and because any contrary principles would involve a form of contradiction. They are indeed judgments of unconditional necessity, in the sense that they imply that what must be done is not necessary because it is a means to some independently valued end, but because the action is a necessary part of a way of life and ideal of conduct. The necessity resides in the nature of the action itself, as specified in the fully explicit moral judgment. The principal and proximate grounds for claiming that the action must, or must not, be performed are to be found in the characterisation of the action offered within the prescription; and if the argument is pressed further, first a virtue or vice, and then a whole way of life will have to be described.

But still a number of distinctions are needed to avoid misunderstandings. First, he who says, for example, 'You must not give a judgment about this until you have heard the evidence', or 'I must stand by my friend in this crisis', claiming an absolute, and unconditional, necessity to act just so on this occasion, is not claiming an overriding necessity so to act in all circumstances and situations. He has so far not generalised at all, as he would have generalised if he were to add 'always' or 'in all circumstances'. The immediate grounds for the necessity of the action or abstention are indicated in the judgment itself. These particular actions, which are cases of the general type 'respecting evidence' and 'standing by friends', are said to be necessary on this occasion in virtue of having just this character, and in virtue of their being this type of action. In other painful circumstances, and on other occasions, other unconditional necessities, with other grounds, might be judged to have overriding claims.

In a situation of conflict, two necessities may be felt to be stringent, and even generally inescapable, and the agent's further reflection may confirm his first feeling of their stringency. Yet in the circumstances of conflict he has to make a choice, and to bring himself to do one of the normally forbidden things, in order to avoid doing the other. He may finally recognise one overriding necessity, even though he would not be ready to generalise it to other circumstances. The necessity that is associated with types of action – e.g. not to betray one's friends – is absolute and unconditional, in the sense that it is not relative to, or conditional upon, some desirable external end: but it is liable occasionally to conflict with other necessities.

A second distinction must be drawn: from the fact that a man thinks that there is nothing other than X which he can decently do in a particular situation it does not follow that it is intuitively obvious to him that he must do X. Certainly he may have reached the conclusion immediately and without reflection; but he might also have reached the very same conclusion after weighing a number of arguments for and against. A person's belief that so-and-so must be done, and that he must not act in any other way, may be the outcome of the calculation of the consequences of not doing the necessary thing: always provided that he sees the avoidance of bringing about these consequences as something that is imposed on him as a necessity in virtue of the character of the situation. The reason for the necessity of the action sometimes is to be found in its later consequences, rather than in the nature and quality of the action evident at the time of action. In every case there will be a description of the action that shows the immediate ground for the necessity, usually by indicating the virtue or vice involved.

Different men, and different social groups, recognise rather different moral necessities in the same essential areas of moral concern. This is no more surprising, or philosophically disquieting, than the fact that different men, and different social groups, will order the primary virtues of men, and the features of an admirable way of life, differently. That the poverty stricken and the desitute must be helped, just because they suffer, and that a great wrong does not demand a great punishment as retribution, are typical modern opinions about what must be done. Reasoning is associated with these opinions, as it is also with the different orderings of essential virtues; there are no conclusive proofs, or infallible intutions, which put a stop to the adducing of new considerations. One does not expect that everyone should recognise the same moral necessities; but rather that everyone should recognise some moral necessities, and similar and overlapping ones, in the same, or almost the same areas, of moral concern.

A man's morality, and the morality of a social group, can properly be seen as falling into two parts, first, a picture of the activities necessary to an ideal way of life which is aspired to, and, second, the unavoidable duties and necessities without which even the elements of human worth, and of a respectworthy way of life, are lacking. The two parts are not rationally unconnected. To take the obvious classical examples: a betrayal of friends in a moment of danger, and for the sake of one's own safety, is excluded from the calculation of possibilities; one may lose perhaps everything else, but this cannot be done; the stain would be too great. And one may take public examples: an outrage of cruelty perpetrated upon undefended civilians in war would constitute a stain that would not be erased and would not be balanced against political success.

How would a sceptical, utilitarian friend of Stephen's, a philosophical friend of the utilitarians, respond to these suggestions? Among other objections he would certainly say that I was turning the clock back, suggesting a return to the moral philosophies of the past: absolute prohibitions, elementary decencies, the recognition of a plurality of prohibitions which do not all serve a single purpose: and with nothing more definite behind them than a form of life aspired to; this is the outline of an Aristotelian ethics: ancient doctrine. Modern utilitarians thought that men have the possibility of indefinite improvement in their moral thinking, and that they were confined and confused by their innate endowments of moral repugnances and emotional admirations. There was a sense of the open future in all their writing. But hope of continuing improvement, if it survives at all now, is now largely without evidence. Lowering the barriers of prohibition, and making rational calculation of consequences the sole foundation of public policies, have so far favoured, and are still favouring, a new callousness in policy, a dullness of sensibility, and sometimes moral despair, at least in respect of public affairs. When the generally respected barriers of impermissible conduct are once crossed, and when no different unconditional barriers, within the same areas of conduct, are put in their place, then the special, apparently superstitious, value attached to the preservation of human life will be questioned. This particular value will no longer be distinguished by an exceptionally solemn prohibition; rather it will be assessed on a common scale alongside other desirable things. Yet it is not clear that the taking of lives can be marked and evaluated on a common scale on which increases of pleasure and diminutions of suffering are also measured. This is the suggested discontinuity which a utilitarian must deny.

Moral prohibitions in general, and particularly those that govern the taking of life, the celebration of the dead, and that govern sexual relations and family relations, are artifices that give human lives some distinctive, peculiar, even arbitrary human shape and pattern. They humanise the natural phases of experience, and lend them a distinguishing sense and direction, one among many possible ones. It is natural for men to expect these artificialities, without which their lives would seem to them inhuman. Largely for this reason a purely naturalistic and utilitarian interpretation of duties and obligations, permissions and prohibitions, in these areas, and particularly in the taking of human life, leaves uneasiness. The idea of morality is connected with the idea that taking human life is a terrible act, which has to be regulated by some set of overriding constraints that constitute a morality; and the connection of ideas alleged here is not a vague one. If there were a people who did not recoil from killing, and, what is a distinguishable matter, who seemed to attach no exceptional value to human life, they would be accounted a community of the subhuman; or, more probably, we would doubt whether their words and practices had been rightly interpreted and whether their way of life had been understood. Yet the taking of life does not have any exceptional importance in utilitarian ethics, that is, in an ethics that is founded exclusively on the actual, ascertained desires and sentiments of men (unlike J. S. Mill's); the taking of life is morally significant in so far as it brings other losses with it. For a strict utilitarian (which J. S. Mill was not) the horror of killing is only the horror of causing other losses, principally of possible happiness; in cases where there are evidently no such losses, the horror of killing becomes superstition. And such a conclusion of naturalism, pressed to its limits, does produce a certain vertigo after reflection. It seems that the mainspring of morality has been taken away.

This vertigo is not principally the result of looking across a century of cool political massacres, undertaken with rational aims; it is also a sentiment with a philosophical thought behind it. A consistent naturalism displaces the pre-reflective moral emphasis upon respect for life, and for the preservation of life, on to an exclusive concern for one or other of the expected future products of being alive – happiness, pleasure, the satisfaction of desires. Respect for human life, independent of the use made of it, may seem to utilitarians a survival of a sacramental consciousness, or at least a survival of a doctrine of the soul's destiny, or of the unique relation between God and man. It had been natural to speak of the moral prohibitions against the taking of life as being respect for the sacredness of an individual life; and this phrase has no proper place, it is very reasonably assumed, in the thought of anyone who has rejected belief in supernatural sanctions.

But the situation may be more complicated. The sacredness of life, so called, and the absolute prohibitions against the taking of life, except under strictly defined conditions, may be admitted to be human inventions. Once the human origin of the prohibitions has been recognised, the prohibition against the taking of life, and respect for human life as such, may still be reaffirmed as absolute. They are reaffirmed as complementary to a set of customs, habits and observances, which are understood by reference to their function, and which are sustained, partly because of, partly in spite of, this understanding: I mean sexual customs, family observances, ceremonial treatment of the dead, gentle treatment of those who are diseased and useless, and of the old and senile, customs of war and treatment of prisoners, treatment of convicted criminals, political and legal safeguards for the rights of individuals, and the customary rituals of respect and gentleness in personal dealings. This complex of habits, and the rituals associated with them, are carried over into a secular morality which makes no existential claims that a naturalist would dispute, and which still rejects the utilitarian morality associated with naturalism. The error of the optimistic utilitarian is that he carries the deritualisation of transactions between men to a point at which men not only can, but ought to, use and exploit each other as they use and exploit any other natural objects, as far as this is compatible with general happiness. And at this point, when the mere existence of an individual person by itself has no value, apart from the by-products and uses of the individual in producing and enjoying desirable states of mind, there is no theoretical barrier against social surgery of all kinds. Not only is there no such barrier in theory: but, more important, the non-existence of the barriers is explicitly recognised. The draining of moral significance from ceremonies, rituals, manners and observances, which imaginatively express moral attitudes and prohibitions, leaves morality incorporated only in a set of propositions and computations: thin and uninteresting propositions, when so isolated from their base in the observances, and manners, which govern ordinary relations with people, and which always manifest implicit moral attitudes and opinions. The computational morality, on which optimists rely, dismisses the non-propositional and unprogrammed elements in morality altogether, falsely confident that these elements can all be ticketed and brought into the computations.

You may object that I now seem to be arguing for the truth of a doctrine by pointing to the evil consequences of its being disbelieved: this is not my meaning. I have been assuming that prohibitions against killing are primary moral prohibitions; secondly, that the customs and rituals that govern, in different societies, relations between the sexes, marriage, property rights, family relationships, and the celebration of the dead, are primary moral customs; they always disclose the peculiar kind of respect for human life, and occasions for disrespect, which a particular people or society recognises, and therefore their more fundamental moral beliefs and attitudes. Ordinarily a cosmology, or metaphysics, is associated with the morality, and, for Europeans, it has usually been a supernatural cosmology. When the supernatural cosmology is generally rejected, or no longer is taken seriously, the idea that human life has a unique value has to be recognised as a human invention. But it is not an invention from nothing at all: the rituals and manners that govern behaviour and respect for persons already express a complex set of moral beliefs and attitudes, and embody a particular way of life. Affirmations of particular rights, duties and obligations, the propositions of a morality, are a development and a correction of this inexplicit morality of ritual and manners.

Each society, each generation within it, and, in the last resort, each reflective individual, accepts, and amends, an established morality expressed in rituals and manners, and in explicit prohibitions; and he will do this, in determining what kind of person he aspires to be and what are the necessary features of a desirable and admirable way of life as he conceives it. If these prohibitions, whatever they are, were no longer observed, and the particular way of life, which depends on them, was lost, and not just amended or replaced, no particular reason would be left to protect human life more than any other natural phenomenon. The different manners of different societies provide, as an element in good manners, for the recognition of differences; so among the more serious moral constraints – serious in the sense that they regulate killing and sexuality and family relationships, and so the conditions of survival of the species – may be the requirement to respect moral differences, at least in certain cases. Provided that there are absolute prohibitions in the same domains with the same function, and provided that their congruence with a desired way of life is grasped, we may without irrationality accept the differences; and there may sometimes be a duty to avoid conflict or to look for compromise in cases of conflict.

Consider the intermediate case between manners in the restricted sense and absolute moral principles: a code of honour of a traditional kind. The different prohibitions of different codes are still recognised as codes of honour; and dishonour incurred in the breach of different disciplines is in each case recognisably dishonour, in virtue of the type of ideal behaviour, and the way of life, that has been betrayed. Prohibitions in other moralities, very different from the moralities of honour, may be similarly diverse in content.

The question cannot be evaded: what is the rational basis for acting as if human life has a peculiar value, quite beyond the value of any other natural things, when one can understand so clearly how different people, for quite different reasons, have come to believe that it has a particular value and to affirm this in their different moralities? Is one not rationally compelled to follow the utilitarians in denying the autonomy of ethics, and the absoluteness of moral prohibitions, if once one comes to understand the social, psychological and other functions which the prohibitions serve? If one reflectively adopts and reaffirms one or other of these moralities, together with its prohibitions, then it may seem that one must be accepting the morality for the sake of its uses and function, rather than for the reasoning associated with it: and this concedes the utilitarian's case.

The conclusion is not necessary. A morality, with its ordering of virtues and its prohibitions, provides a particular ideal of humanity in an ideal way of life; and this moral ideal explains where and why killing is allowed and also for what purposes a man might reasonably give his life; and in this sense it sets its own peculiar value on human life. One cannot doubt that there are causes, largely unknown, that would explain why one particular ideal has a hold upon men at a particular time and place, apart from the reasoning that they would use to defend it. And it seems certain that the repugnances and horror surrounding some moral prohibitions are sentiments that have both a biological and a social function. But the attitude of a reflective man to these repugnances and prohibitions does not for this reason have to be a utilitarian one. One may on reflection respect and reaffirm the prohibitions, and the way of life that they protect, for reasons unconnected with their known or presumed functions: just as one may respect and adopt a code of manners, or a legal system, for reasons that are unconnected with the known functions of such codes and systems in general, and unconnected also with the known causes that brought these particular codes and systems into existence. The reasons that lead a reflective man to prefer one code of manners, and one legal system, to another must be moral reasons; that is, he must find his reasons in some order of priority of interests and activities in the kind of life that he praises and admires and that he aspires to have, and in the kind of person that he wants to become. Reasons for the most general moral choices, which may sometimes be choices among competing moralities, must be found in philosophical reasoning, if they are found at all: that is, in considerations about the relation of men to the natural, or to the supernatural, order.

I will mention one inclining philosophical reason, which has in the past been prominent in moral theories, particularly those of Aristotle and of Spinoza, and which influences me. One may on reflection find a particular set of prohibitions and injunctions, and a particular way of life protected by them, acceptable and respectworthy, partly because this specifically conceived way of life, with its accompanying prohibitions, has in history appeared natural, and on the whole still feels natural, both to oneself and to others. If there are no overriding reasons for rejecting this way of life, or for rejecting some distinguishing features of it, its felt and proven naturalness is one reason among others for accepting it. This reason is likely to influence particularly those who, unlike utilitarians, cannot for other reasons believe that specific states of mind of human beings are the only elements of value in the universe: who, on the contrary, believe that the natural order as a whole is the fitting object of that kind of unconditional interest and respect that is called moral: that the peculiar value to be attached to human life, and the prohibitions against the taking of life, are not dependent on regarding and treating human beings as radically different from other species in some respects that cannot be specified in plain, empirical statements: that the exceptional value attached both to individual lives, and to the survival of the species as a whole, resides in the power of the human mind to begin to understand, and to enjoy, the natural order as a whole, and to reflect upon this understanding and enjoyment: and that, apart from this exceptional power, the uncompensated destruction of any species is always a loss to be avoided.

Among Leslie Stephen's near contemporaries George Eliot and

George Henry Lewes had accepted a variant of Spinozistic naturalism close to the doctrine that I have been suggesting. But they still believed in the probability of future moral improvements, once superstitions had gone. Their ethics was still imbued with an optimism that was certainly not shared by Spinoza, and with a sense of an open and unconfined future for the species. Spinoza's own naturalism was quite free from optimism about the historical future. He did not suggest that advanced, highly educated societies will for the first time be governed largely by the dictates of reason, and that human nature will radically change, and that the conflict between reason and the incapacitating emotions will be largely resolved. Rather he suggests an opposing view of history and of the future: that moral progress, in the proper sense of the increasing dominance of gentleness and of reason, is not to be expected except within very narrow limits. He thought that he knew that as psycho-physical organisms persons are so constructed that there must always in most men be recurrences of unreason alongside reason, and that in this respect social and historical change would be superficial in their consequences. This pessimism, or at least lack of optimism, is compatible with a secular doctrine, akin to that of natural law, which represents many of the seemingly natural prohibitions of non-computational morality as more likely to be endorsed than to be superseded by reflection. A naturalist of his persuasion does not foresee a future in which rational computation will by itself replace the various imaginations, unconscious memories and habits, rituals and manners, which have lent substance and content to men's moral ideas, and which have partly formed their various ways of life.

Some of these ways of life, and certainly their complexity and variety, may be respected as an aspect of natural variety: and, like other natural phenomena, they may over the years be studied and explained, at least to some degree explained. From this point of view, that of natural knowledge, the species, if it survives, may perhaps make interesting advances. But this was not the utilitarians' hope; they looked for an historical transformation of human nature, through new moral reasoning, and this has not occurred and is now not to be reasonably expected.

2 Public and Private Morality

STUART HAMPSHIRE

1

In the Leslie Stephen lecture, re-printed as 'Morality and Pessimism', I used the phrase 'rational computational morality' in a pejorative sense, and I spoke of the 'abstract cruelty in politics' which had been associated in the U.S.A. during the Vietnam War with a new quasi-quantitative precision in the calculation of the consequences of alternative policies. These charges against a type of utilitarian thinking need fully argued support, and particularly the use of 'rational' here and of 'abstract' needs to be explained. Why should 'rational' be used in an abusive sense? It was perhaps evident that I was drawing on an Aristotelian idea of the form of rationality which is involved in practical reasoning. There is a presumed distinction between rationality in choosing between lines of conduct, practical reason, and rationality in arriving at true statements and beliefs, theoretical reason; and this distinction is associated with a specific account of practical reasoning. Within this account the word 'abstract', when applied to practical reasoning, becomes a reproach and for several distinct reasons. These reasons I shall set out as distinctly as I can. Even the word 'rational', as it occurs in the phrase 'rational computational morality', can be part of a reproach, because of the implication that the wrong model of rationality is involved: wrong, in the sense that it is inappropriate to practical reasoning, even if it is appropriate to reasoning of other kinds.

2

I shall borrow from Aristotle that emphasis on the normal condensation of practical reasoning which makes it resemble perception, or, more strictly, perceptual identification. I can tell that the man in the distance coming towards us is Jones, and there is an answer to the question 'how did I tell?', even if I do not know the answer and even if I never will know. The presumption behind the question is that I had a way of telling. I might have told who he was by the way he walked, or, more specifically, by a nameable feature of the way he walked; or I might have told by the clothes he was wearing, visible in the distance, which sagged in a characteristic way. There is an indefinite variety of ways in which I might have told, some being more reliable, and better, ways of telling than others. I might have arrived at the right conclusion – that the man was Jones – and yet my way of arriving at this conclusion might have been a bad way because a generally unreliable one. For example, perhaps he was wearing, as it happened, someone else's clothes, and the look was in fact quite untypical of him, even though I had thought it typical. I had a reason for my conclusion, but a bad one that happened to produce good results: as will sometimes happen with bad ways of doing things.

A way of telling on a particular occasion that so-and-so is a so-and-so in a perceptual situation can plausibly be represented as the route which the subject followed to the conclusion on that occasion. If he travelled the route very fast and unself-consciously, and without communicating with anybody, it may be that he will be quite unable to tell how he arrived at the conclusion, when he is asked. On the other hand perhaps he does remember immediately that first he noticed such-and-such a feature and from that concluded immediately that it was Jones; and he remembers that no other feature of the person consciously influenced him, or consciously influenced him to the same degree. He is the authority, though a fallible one, and he is in the best position to judge what his reasoning was, if it was the kind of explicit reasoning which can be remembered. He is also in the best position to judge whether it was of this explicit kind, though in neither case is his judgment infallible or incorrigible. But very often he does not know and cannot say, when asked, what noticed features of the object caused him to reach the conclusion that he did about its identity. Vast background knowledge was called into play, and no one feature was salient.

I am recalling a very general feature of human activity and

functioning. It is a familiar fact that most of my routine actions are performed without my knowing how I perform them, unless I come up against a difficulty in performing them. I do not know, or need to know, which muscles I use, or what pressures I exert, while riding a bicycle, unless I am going up a steep hill, or unless I am engaged in a race, when the maximum performance is the end in view. When I am merely bicycling from place to place in the ordinary way, I do not monitor my performance self-consciously and I would probably be unable to say how the particular performance was carried through: 'I just bicycled, as I always do' would be the natural answer. This is what I would also say about my identification of Jones, in cases where there was no difficulty and where there was no contest and when my powers of identifying were not being tested.

The reasoning that enters into perceptual identifications are to be compared with very ordinary and very often repeated types of action involving bodily movements; in adults, the actions are normally condensed into routines performed unselfconsciously and without awareness of distinct stages and steps. The stages and steps involved are sometimes brought to consciousness, and their existence revealed, in circumstances of difficulty and of breakdown. The stages and steps will also be brought to light when the activity is being taught to beginners or to the handicapped. In the process of learning, the many stages and steps, at first taken deliberately and one by one, gradually become internalised and are finally not only unnoticed but practically unnoticeable. When the learning is finished and the performance fully internalised, the subject no longer even thinks of the performance as having stages and steps, unless he runs into difficulties, and not necessarily even then.

The reasoning that enters into perceptual identification, both of types and of individuals, is probably the commonest of all types of reasoning, and therefore the most thoroughly learnt and fully internalised. Aristotle makes the comparison between perceptual judgment, and the reasoning entering into it, and practical choice in substantial moral issues, and the reasoning entering into that, when he wants to stress the the internalisation of norms of conduct in the experienced man of settled dispositions. It is evidently a partial parallel, but it holds for Aristotle's limited purposes. It may be supplemented by parallels with other cases of condensed reasoning which are closer to the reasoning that enters into moral judgment and into substantial moral decisions.

Consider the rules, conventions, and habits of behaviour which fall under the broad heading of manners, that is, social manners in any society and social group. Manners are apt to be:

(1) learnt both by precept and by example

(2) finally habitual, unconsidered, and wholly internalised

(3) applied in particular situations which are immediately recognised as falling under a certain convention-invoking descriptions, and both this recognition, and also the choice of behaviour to which it leads, involve condensed reasoning. There is a fourth characteristic of the choice of behaviour to be noted;

(4) in difficult situations of conflict of conventions, or of rules, of good manners, situations which are normally not too common, the subject has to make his choice of behaviour explicit to himself, and also to make explicit the reasoning which supports his conclusion.

Manners provide a close parallel to the morals of private life in the relation of implicit and explicit reasoning to conduct. Our patterns of behaviour, from infancy onwards, are permeated by explicitly learnt, and by imitated, rituals and set forms of address in more or less finely discriminated social situations and family situations. There is a large overlapping, even in modern societies, between the claims of good manners and moral claims.

We do normally have reasons for the modification of our behaviour in situations in accordance with accepted manners, even if we are totally unable to say what these reasons are, when we are asked; that is, 'He has a reason for behaving in such-and-such a manner in such-and-such situations' does not entail either 'He is now able to say why he behaves as he does', or even 'He would recognise the correct account of why he behaves as he does, if it were suggested to him.' He might have learnt, by imitating his elders, to adapt his behaviour to changing situations in accordance with rules and conventions which have never been explicitly stated to him, and even according to rules which have never been explicitly stated at all.

Suppose that he has learnt by imitation over a long period of time to adapt his posture and mode of address to fit the different sex, age, and social standing of the persons whom he meets. When he makes a mistake, and behaves unfittingly, his mistake is described with the minimum of generality: e.g. 'She is an old woman, and the wife of a relation of yours, so why did you behave so casually?' He has learnt his variations of behaviour in the same way that he learnt to speak his native language: by imitating others and by being corrected, with greater or less generality, when he goes wrong. He need not have learnt a code of manners, explicitly formulated, any more than he need have learnt the rules of grammar applicable to his native tongue. In both cases one could speak of the rules and conventions being internalised.

I have chosen as an example manners to compare with morality, in respect of internalised rules and conventions, because manners are near to morals on the one side and akin to language on the other side. It is generally held to be a positive advantage that manners should be internalised, and that a man should not need to consult a remembered code-book, or a set of instructions, in order to be sure how he should behave in various situations. Manners should be 'natural', it is said, or should be 'instinctive'. The implication is that the correct behaviour should not be the outcome of careful and laborious calculation and reflection; it should be immediate, spontaneous, governed by intuition. Something similar would be claimed for the proper command of a language; one should be able to speak spontaneously and intuitively, and to select the right word without reflection and without recourse to dictionary or grammar. Also the swift and intuitive choice of the right words is often a matter of good manners and sometimes also a moral matter; for instance, as clearly expressing the right feeling.

Aristotle allowed very little difference in this respect between morality and good manners. Both should be fully internalised as stable dispositions which lead, effortlessly and immediately, to reasonable conduct and to reasonable assessments of situations demanding action, and to making the assessments without too much brooding and effort. He specifically compares acting from a stable disposition with the effortless correct use of language; it is not sufficient to do what the grammatical man does. One must do it in the same way.

Is there, and must there be, a difference between manners and morals in this one specific respect: that the rules of good manners, generally speaking, are, among other things, necessarily internalised, and, in this sense, should become natural, while no such implication holds for the rational man whose conduct, in politics or private life, is morally admirable? Is this a valid contrast? As soon as the question is posed, it is evident that different moral theories yield different answers to the question and that our pre-theoretical intuitions are not decisive. Aristotelian theory entails that there is no very significant difference between manners and morals in this respect, and this is part of the reason, within the theory, why there is for him no ultimate divergence in the normal run of things between a morally admirable life and a satisfying and happy one; for to the man who is rational in substantial practical matters it has become second nature to act rightly and he does so more or less effortlessly and as a matter of course and with pleasure. The most significant advantages of explicitness in moral reasoning are that explicit knowledge of the reasons why (a) is in itself an intellectual virtue, and (b) explicit knowledge of the reasons why is necessary for the man who takes a leading part in public life and in affairs of state. He has to explain and recommend his policies to others. (c) Explicit reasoning is more open to being checked and confusions in reasoning are in general more likely to be noticed.

There is no implication within Kantian theory that the imperatives which practical reason must follow are internalised except in the man of holy will; and there is certainly no implication that the imperatives of morality are to be compared with, or essentially resemble, the imperatives of a code of manners. The implication is very much the reverse: good manners require accurate discrimination between variously different social situations in a minutely observant spirit, and they do not require high-level generalisations.

The contrast can be represented as that between noticing a great number and variety of independently variable features of particular situations on the one hand, and on the other hand bringing a few, wholly explicit principles to bear upon situations, which have to be subsumed under the principles, as in some kinds of legal reasoning. Kant was assimilating important practical reasoning and decision-making to laying down the law, rather as

God does, or did, lay down the law. Aristotle assimilated political decision-making, and practical reasoning generally, to the condensed, trained judgment of particular situations by games-players, craftsmen, performers of all kinds. Evidently these are assimilations only, not claimed identities; but the difference between the assimilations is significant. Different models of rationality in practical reasoning are implied by the assimilations.

Like the rules and conventions of language, the rules and conventions of good manners need to be codified, or at least to be well understood, because they govern transactions between persons and they require conformity in response. The responses need to be, in the most strict sense, regular and expected. There is advantage in their being habitual, and in their being inbuilt, reliable dispositions; the less brooding on difficult cases the better for social ease and harmony. More fundamentally, codes of manners, like languages, are essentially various, serving to distinguish different social groups. Any one social group may in fact believe that its good manners are the only good manners, and that its good manners ought ideally to be recognised by all groups as constituting good manners. Anyone who seriously makes this claim, and who supports it with argument, and who argues that other conceptions of good manners are in some way mistaken or inferior, is in effect claiming that his good manners are a proper part of morality. He has crossed the uncertain frontier between manners and morality, as they are now recognised, when he makes the claim that there is a good reason why everyone ought to behave as his particular norm of good manners prescribes, whether these are the manners of a man's social group or not. If there is a right way to behave to which all men are required to conform, and if there is some coherent reason why this behaviour is required of all men, it is difficult to see how the label 'moral' could be withheld from this requirement.

3

Does right conduct in public and private life alike, and judged from a serious moral point of view, constantly require explicit thought, and the careful weighing of arguments, and the making of calculations? Most utilitarian moralists will say that rationality in practical reasoning, where serious moral issues are concerned, is incompatible with habitual responses and internalised dispositions; in the context of practical reason on moral issues, rationality entails constant calculation, and specifically calculation of consequences. This calculation may be performed rapidly and habitually, but always the calculation can be, and ought to be, reconstructed and made explicit. This is the position that must be examined. Is it a necessary condition of a man being rational in his practical decisions that he should be able, in some appropriate setting, to give a satisfactory account of his reasons? Shall we have to say, in a serious moral case, that his decision was irrational, in a bad sense, if he is unable to explain his decision as the conclusion of a calculation, and of a calculation that is respectable? The Aristotelian analogy with perception is used to suggest that it does not follow from the fact that a man does not know what his reasons were for a decision just taken that there were no good reasons, and that he acted under the influence of causes that do not count as reasons; for instance, that he acted without thought or impulsively, or as an unthinking response to some stimulus, or because he just wanted to, when the desire was an unthinking one. It is not essential to being a reason that the thought that constitutes a reason should be accessible, under favourable conditions, to the consciousness of the thinker and agent.

The principal argument for this conclusion starts from a philosophical premise, which in *Thought and Action* I dubbed the inexhaustibility of description. Any situation which confronts me, and which is not a situation in a game, has an inexhaustible set of discriminable features over and above those which I explicitly notice at the time because they are of immediate interest to me. Secondly, the situation has features over and above those which are mentionable within the vocabulary that I possess and use. I 'take in' the situation, noticing the features that are particularly relevant to my interests at the time, and I respond to it in accordance with my prevailing desires and purposes and my prevailing beliefs and knowledge about the means to satisfy them. The reasons for my actions and conduct, when the actions are voluntary and intended, are to be found in my contemporary desires, current or standing, in my beliefs and knowledge, taken together. My desires and interests form a vast system, and only a few of them are called into play at any one time. Of many of them I would not know how strong they were, or even that they existed, until some situation requiring carefully considered action brings them to my attention. Only a very few of them are desires formed after reflection and therefore explicitly recognised at birth. As for the system of my beliefs, it is evident that there is in my mind a vast store of unsurveyable background knowledge and belief; and against this background my specific beliefs about the present situation form themselves.

When it comes to giving an account of the reasons for an action, or course of conduct, one picks out a few salient desires and beliefs from the foreground of consciousness and, more specifically, those that distinguish this particular occasion and this particular person: the ordinary, run-of-the-mill desires and beliefs are not worth mentioning. Even in the case of action following upon fully explicit deliberation, and of a contemporary account of the reasons for the decision, the reasons are a selection of the interesting items, and are recognised as being a selection. Just as I am only aware of a small selection of the features of the situation confronting me, so I am only aware of a small selection of the desires and beliefs which, if altered, would probably alter my conduct.

The parallel with language is useful. It has so far proved impossible to design a translating machine which takes account of the indefinite variety of contexts, linguistic and external, in which a given form of words is used; and normally the contexts affect the sense. However elaborate the programme built into the machine, it is apt to fall short, if only because of the sheer unpredictable variety of contexts encountered. The variety is not only humanly unpredictable but humanly unimaginable. Yet a person translating immediately sees the recurring form of words against the background of a different context and then intuitively makes the required adjustment to the sense. A person is a complex mechanism naturally designed over a long evolutionary period to make such adjustments.

For every choice of words that a translator makes in a particular context while translating, there is a complex of reasons, good or bad, which might account for the choice made; reasons drawn from the context, from the associations of the words remembered from the past, from the syntax of the speaker or writer, and so forth. A very experienced and successful translator might be unable to give the reasons that had led him to choose one word as the appropriate translation rather than another which is nearly synonymous. But he might be quite sure that there were reasons for the choice, which were his reasons, and that the choice was not an unthinking one. If he did reflect on the reasons for his choice, trying to evaluate them, he would normally have at least the following difficulties: the reasons that he gives would be the salient contexts, selected parallel passages and associations, picked out from the unrecoverable complex of his verbal memories of uses of these and of similar words. On reflection these selected contexts seem to him to have been present to his mind and in the foreground of his awareness, but against a huge background of other contexts and associations determining his decision, but not now recalled. He has no method, even in principle, of individuating the reasons determining his decision, and therefore of arriving at any exact causal statement, or any complete one. He could not remember the great number of obvious and undistinguished contexts in which he has encountered the words in question and which have finally given him a 'feeling', as one might say, for the possible standard employments of the words.

The skill in translating of a man who knows two languages well resides in a great accumulation of preconscious memories. That the memories should be preconscious, or unconscious, is a natural advantage because speed and fluency are of the essence of linguistic skills. There is little advantage for a translator in possessing the rather different skill which would be involved in giving an adequate account of the distinct reasons for his choice of equivalents. This advantage would exist if in normal circumstances a public defence of the decisions was required, and if the translations had to be publicly justified, before they could be accepted as adequate translations. Even in those imaginary circumstances the justification would fall short of being complete, for the reasons already given, and there would be residuary appeals to particular forms of words 'sounding right', also to associations of words which cannot be precisely distinguished and listed. The reason-giving would generally tail off into mere intuition, with claims of 'not sounding the same' and of 'seeming to fit'; and there would be appeals to the translator's accumulation of linguistic experience as in itself a kind of reason for accepting his decision as correct.

The analogy between decisions in translating from language to language, and the intuitions of rightness involved, and on the other side decisions about the right conduct in a situation requiring judgment is, first, an analogy in respect of multiplicity of uncountable background features normally involved in the deciding mind; secondly, in respect of the mind's ability, in sophisticated actions as in routine movements, to draw upon a vast store of memories which are preconscious; thirdly, in respect of the thinking that is in both cases highly condensed, and that is not for this reason to be reconstructed easily, as amounting to arguments which could be used in conclusive support of the decisions.

The skilled use of language is an extreme case of condensed and unreconstructible thinking, and our thinking about political and moral issues neither normally is, nor normally ought to be, to the same degree condensed and unreconstructible. Emotions lead to confusions in moral reasoning and a measure of explicitness is to some degree a safeguard against confusion so caused. But the extreme case of the translator's skill in choice of words illustrates that element in practical thinking on serious moral issues which a 'computational morality' either ignores or means to banish. The need for a reconstruction of the reasons for a decision, and for using that reconstruction as a part of a justification of the decision, is often to be expected where serious moral issues are confronted; and for this reason alone the analogy with language cannot be pressed too far. There is a difference of degree. But the analogy with law, which is usually invoked to illuminate reasoning about moral questions, also cannot be pressed too far in the opposite direction. The thought that enters into a legal decision must always be reconstructible as a potential argument in further justification of that decision. There must also be a known record of earlier relevant cases and decisions, and not a confused memory of an indefinite multiplicity of parallel cases.

That in the absence of difficulty and uncertainty, and when there is no discussion between persons, reasoning about conduct should be normally unreflective and implicit is an obvious advantage to the species. Over much of its range practical reason has to replace the largely inflexible and the largely predetermined responses and routines of animal behaviour. We have to think fast in the exercise of many skills which involve feeling and good judgment. Often we must not spend too much energy on reflection, where love and friendship are at risk.

You may now ask: what is the philosophical importance of this fact of the internalisation of thinking processes? Why is it worth while to dwell on it, and to underline it? Part of the answer is: because there is a philosophical tradition which identifies the ideal of rationality with explicitness in moving from reasons to conclusions; and it is a very respectable tradition, traceable to Plato. Undeniably there are good reasons for associating rationality, as an ideal to be aimed at, with some degree of explicitness in moving from reasons to conclusions in difficult cases, and when justice and public policies are in question. But rationality ought not to be identified with explicitness.

The tradition is that to know why the moral claims that seem to us intuitively right are really right is to be able to show that they form a coherent system. Then the moral claims have the backing of reason, while our intuitions may be coloured by variable sentiments. After the discovery of coherence the moral claims are more secure, in a psychological sense, than they were before; that is the first advantage. The second traditional advantage is that some intuitions are rightly corrected when the stabilising theory is fully understood; doubtful cases of moral claims are clarified and classified clearly within the theory, and conflict between claims are rendered intelligible by the theory, which explains why the conflicts must arise and how they are to be solved. Without the theory there is no clear method of distinguishing between a moral claim and a prejudice or superstition, and of isolating a mere effect of custom and habit. The theory must accord with the main run of moral claims which are recognised as binding, and it will at the same time explain why a few claims have come to seem binding, which, when examined systematically, are seen not to be. This is one traditional view of the value of moral theory. It associates rationality in moral judgment with coherence, which in turn implies an absence of irresoluble conflicts between moral claims. Rationality has exactly the same sense, and the same application, as in theoretical inquiries; the theory that guides the beliefs of the rational man should exclude unresolved conflicts between claims and should be comprehensive, covering all types of contingency. On the other hand intuitions, however carefully reflected upon, may at any time lead to irresoluble conflicts in practical judgment, prescribing two incompatible courses of conduct as equally necessary and as equally required of any morally respect-worthy man.

Science and law require as institutions public and argumentative justifications and a publicly defensible consistency. Irresoluble conflicts and incompatibility cannot be tolerated; not only that, but there is a requirement of a general and recognised method for resolving any apparently irresoluble conflicts and contradictions that arise. Consequently anyone thinking, alone and silently, about a scientific or a legal problem is thinking about the reasons he would give, if challenged, for any particular conclusion which his intuitions suggest is correct. He would not even allow his intuitive judgment to constitute his conclusion unless he could formulate, at least in outline, the reasons that he would cite in public argument; and the reasons would show the coherence of the judgment in question with a set of already accepted propositions. The private thought, the silent deliberation, take place under the shadow of the public institution.

If there is no shadow of the public and institutional test of a type of conclusion, and if a man is deeply concerned with the particular case before him and in being careful in his conclusion about it; if he is thinking alone, and if he is not particularly interested in proving to others that he has the right solution; under these conditions, the concept of rationality that is tied to giving satisfactory reasons will have a weaker hold on him. He will not be compelled, by the very nature of his interest, to be sure that any conclusion that he reaches is supported by sufficient reasons and that he has a convincing argument ready, if he is challenged. He will not necessarily need to make his inferences explicit, though he may wish to do so for reasons of his own unconnected with public institutions. He may want to check that he has not 'leapt to a conclusion', following some association of ideas: to check that he is not believing his conclusion principally because he wants to believe it. A connoisseur attributes works of art to their right sources and infers their dates. He detects fakes, copies, the works of disciples and followers. He knows the real thing, lots of different kinds of real thing, within the range of his experience and study; but he is not usually able to say how he tells. Connoisseurs in countless other fields, apart from works of art, are in the same position; able to discriminate with consistent success, but not knowing at all precisely how they do it, not knowing what makes them arrive at the conclusion, usually the right one; having no explicitly formulated method which they are applying with any consciousness of what it is. They know that, like the translator, they are guided by a weight of experience of many similar cases and by many associations and memories, not all of which they can disentangle and recall. The memories are too extensive to be accessible, but methodically stored and linked by a causality which they do not understand and which is too complex to trace. The connoisseur – of drawings, of horses, of wines, of the wind and weather at sea – needs to concentrate on noticing unexpected features and on using his senses and on being open to impressions, and on being receptive to unexpected inputs, which may change his judgment. Negatively, he must not impose a ready-made rational structure on his observations, if this entails attending to ordinarily expected features of the object, and attending only with set ideas of what is relevant.

The connoisseur may never know, and be able to distinguish, the separate steps, or the separate inputs, which led him to his conclusion, and he may never be able to put his inference into any standard form. Another example – the inferences that lead one to understand the sentences of one's own language spoken by a foreigner in a strange accent are very complex and very efficient; but there would usually be no way of reconstructing the inferences that led to the conclusion in a standard order.

4

On what grounds do I argue that, in decisions of substantial moral concern, inferences of the intuitive kind have a proper place alongside inferences of the explicit and fully articulated kind? That

we ought sometimes, even in serious issues of public policy, to
follow our intuitions of what is best to be done, in spite of the
fact that in some cases we cannot specify a convincing set of
reasons to support the intuitions?

A defender of rationality in practical reasoning, in the traditional
sense of 'rational', may admit that it is often difficult, and sometimes impossible, to make fully explicit the reasons for a decision
made in a substantial moral issue. But he may argue that one ought
to aim at full explicitness in specifying the principal reasons for
a judgment in any serious moral issue, even if one does not
succeed in disentangling every separate consideration that influenced the outcome. Following Aristotle, this defender of rationality of the traditional kind will argue that the policy of evaluating
explicitly every consideration influencing him is a guarantee
against confusions about the ends of action, misleading associations, subjective impressions, sentimental prejudice and superstition; and this is a sufficient vindication of traditional rationality
in moral reasoning, quite apart from the occasional necessity of
publicly defending a decision. The more careful and methodical
the deliberation before action, with an explicit reviewing of
arguments and counter-arguments, the less likely a man is to be
misled by received opinions and mere confusions of thought.

To summarise the arguments in reply: the mind is an
instrument developed by natural selection to identify objects, to
learn and to speak languages, to perform an immense range of
routine actions, to recognise and to respond appropriately and with
feeling to persons and to form attachments to them, and to enter
into all the interchanges of social life. It is also an instrument for
abstract thought, and, more specifically, for learning mathematics
and for grasping legal distinctions. In the abusive phrase 'abstract
computational morality' the word 'abstract' is there for good
reason. As abstraction has its natural and proper place in reasoning, so does its contrary, which is the mind's openness to a great
range of largely unexpected observed features of a situation all
of which are allowed to influence the response. Kant's account of
practical reason was an insistence on the abstract will, which in
virtue of its rationality would not be engaged by the multiplicity
of concrete features that complicate particular situations. In virtue

of its rationality Kant's practical reason, at least in serious moral issues, will conceive situations abstractly with a view to subsuming them under the relevant moral principle.

An opposing school of moralists, utilitarians, associate rationality in moral reasoning with scientific method, therefore with verifiable judgments of right and wrong, and therefore with a general criterion or test that yields definite results in particular cases. Therefore a primary abstraction is required, as in any applied science, an abstraction that leaves out of account in practical deliberation those features of situations which are not mentioned in the utilitarian calculus. The agent can feel secure with his rational method. He has eliminated the worst uncertainties of living and he is left with manageable empirical calculations; and these are the kind of calculation which every prudent and efficient man makes every day, fitting accessible means to desired ends. Much that is puzzling, exceptional and difficult about those practical questions which are called moral issues has been cleared away for the utilitarian by a policy of abstraction.

5

If I were to defend further the case against abstract thinking in many matters of moral judgment, and against abstract thinking in the conduct of public affairs, I would do best to tell true stories, drawn from direct experience, of events which have actually involved difficult decisions. Some of the decisions would be matters of public policy, and the agent would have a public and a representative role complicating the decision for him. Some of the decisions would arise from tangled situations in private life, and the story would need to describe fully and carefully the dispositions and feelings and history of the persons involved. Telling the stories, with the facts taken from experience and not filleted and at second hand, imposes some principles of selection. One has to decide what the story is and what the situation is, or was, from the point of view of morality. In telling the story one has to select the facts and probabilities which, taken together, constitute the situation confronting the agent. If the story is well told, nothing that is relevant to the decision is left out and not much that is irrelevant to the decision is included in the story; there should be no further questions to be asked about the circumstances before a decision about the right course of action is made, or before a past decision is judged to be right or wrong.

Gradually, and by accumulation of examples drawn from experience, belief that the features of the particular case, indefinite in number, are not easily divided into the morally relevant and morally irrelevant will be underlined by the mere process of story-telling.

One cannot establish conclusively by argument in general terms the general conclusion that the morally relevant features of situations encountered cannot be circumscribed. One cannot prove by a prior argument that one does not actually employ a definite criterion of right conduct, specifying a closed set of morally relevant features. One can only appeal to actual examples and call the mind back to personal experience, which will probably include occasions when the particular circumstances of the case modified what would have been the expected and principled decisions, and for reasons which do not themselves enter into any recognised principle.

When lecturing on moral philosophy, I used often to tell a true story of a wartime experience to illustrate moral conflict and to suggest to others that such conflicts are a common experience, and also that they constitute the essence of moral problems, as they are known in most public roles. The episode involved the interrogation of a captured spy, and my difficulty in deciding how he should be treated. The theoretical interest in the story-telling was always in the selection of the circumstances surrounding the interrogation which ought to be included in the story if the complexity of the original moral problem was to be fully repro-duced. I noticed that on different occasions, and without any clear intention, I tended to stress different features in the situation as relevant to the problem, and that I did not always even include the same elements of the situation, as belonging to the story. Even to speak of 'elements of the situation' and 'features' as included in the story is to oversimplify by a false individuation. I described the episode in different words on different occasions, always under the necessity of omitting some of the circumstances which another person might reasonably consider relevant to the decision. There are always dangers in circumscribing a lived-through situation and in converting it into a definite and clearly stated problem. So often one thinks or says, from the standpoint of the agent: 'So much that mattered has been left out of the story; it was not quite as simple as that.'

The point about false individuation, stressed in *Thought and Action*, is fundamental in the argument against abstraction. Just as we may mislead ourselves by representing situations confronting us as constituted by a definite and final set of elements, so we may also mislead ourselves by representing a tract of our behaviour as constituted by a definite set of distinct actions; how the behaviour over a period of time is broken up into distinct actions is often not unproblematical, even apart from the familiar fact that the same action usually admits of many different descriptions, and that the differences are often relevant to moral judgment. An abstract morality places a prepared grid upon conduct and upon a person's activities and interests, and thereafter one only tends to see the pieces of his conduct and life as they are divided by lines on the grid. From the standpoint of morality, a sceptical nominalism is an aid to careful thinking.

6

There is another, altogether different reason for rejecting any rational morality, and moral theory, which could be described as 'abstract and computational'. This is the claim that it is of the essence of moral problems that on occasion they seem hopeless, incapable of solution, leaving no right action open; this has been an objection not only to utilitarianism of any form, but to any exactly prescribed moral ideal.

We ordinarily encounter serious moral problems as conflicts between moral claims which, considered *a priori*, seem absolute and exceptionless and which are in fact irreconcilable in the situations that present the problem. Unless one has decided in advance that only one feature of situations is ever of moral concern (for instance, happiness), such situations of conflict between absolute moral claims will occasionally occur and are not to be avoided. Moral theories may be invoked to disguise and to gloze over the conflicts by a variety of strategies: for instance, by denying that the conflicting claims are really absolute claims, or by denying that there is in the long run, and taking a life as a whole, an ultimate conflict. One ideal of rationality requires that behind the apparent conflicts there should be an overall coherence between moral claims and between the most sought after and praised dispositions of men; they are the necessary constituents of the one supremely desirable way of life.

'Absolute' in 'absolute moral claims' needs explanation. A moral claim, which may be a duty or a right or an obligation, is absolute when it is not conditional upon, or subordinate to, any further moral claim or purpose. A course of action is absolutely forbidden, or absolutely enjoined, if the prohibition or requirement is not conditional upon the presence of any features not mentioned in the prohibition or injunction. The prohibition or injunction contains its own sense, and explains itself. That justice should be done, and should be seen to be done, in a criminal trial is an absolute requirement within the moral convictions of many people, though not of all people: that is, many people believe that, if there is a trial, justice is absolutely required, and this is required irrespective of the circumstances surrounding the trial and irrespective of consequences. Other persons, for example, most utilitarians, would argue that the requirement is a conditional one, and not absolute; good consequences are essential and the requirement would lapse in view of the disastrous consequences of justice in a particular case. That torture of prisoners of any kind under any circumstances is morally wrong is an absolute prohibition within the moral principles of many people. But some would regard it as a conditional prohibition; they might say that in fact there are probably no circumstances in which, all things considered and allowing for the effect of example, torture of prisoners does not in the long run add to the sum of suffering and is permissible. But they would argue that, if there were such circumstances, then the requirement would lapse, because the wrongness comes from the suffering.

Two features of moral claims need to be distinguished: (a) a moral claim may be absolute in the sense indicated, namely, that there are no circumstances in which it lapses and ceases to be a moral requirement; (b) a moral claim may be absolute, and yet may come into conflict with another absolute moral claim, with the consequence that one of them is in the final decision overridden, even though it has not lapsed.

That a man must not be declared guilty on a criminal charge and punished unless he has been offered legal aid, and unless due process has been observed, may be considered an absolute prohibition, even though it is conditional in form. It would not be an absolute prohibition if there were cicumstances, not mentioned in the prohibition itself, in which the prohibition would lapse and cease to exist: for example, if the prohibition ceased to exist as soon as the suffering directly caused by observing it clearly exceeded the bad effects of undermining this just rule.

I have elsewhere[1] argued that we naturally think, when uncorrupted by theory, of a multiplicity of moral claims, which sometimes come into conflict with each other, just as we think of a multiplicity of human virtues, which sometimes come into conflict with each other; so much so, that if one hears that someone has a moral problem, one immediately assumes that he is confronted with just such a difficult conflict of claims. It is typical and essential, not marginal and accidental, that moral reasoning should be concerned with such conflicts. Unavoidable conflict of principles of conduct, and not a harmony of purposes, is the stuff of morality, as we ordinarily experience it, and unless we resolve after reflection to impose a harmony by allowing only one overriding principle of conduct.

'Overriding', like 'absolute', is a word that requires explanation, if there is to be an intelligible distinction between a moral claim that lapses, and ceases to exist, under certain conditions and a moral claim that is overridden. One may have a moral obligation to assist one's partner in a joint enterprise when he calls on one in difficulties; but this obligation may lapse, and cease to exist, if he later makes it clear that he no longer wishes to incur such an obligation on his side. This situation of lapse is to be contrasted with a situation in which your obligation to assist your partner is in unexpected circumstances overridden by urgent considerations

[1] 'Morality and Pessimism' (Chapter 1) and *Two Theories of Morality* (Oxford 1977).

of public policy, which imposes duties of overriding importance on you, duties that cannot be fulfilled if your obligation is to be fulfilled. There is a conflict, and one is pulled in two different directions by moral claims that remain in force. The obligation does not lapse, or cease to exist; nothing has happened which removes its basis and nullifies or cancels it. Equally in the familiar case of a conflict of absolute duties, for instance, a conflict between the duty to be impartial and just in adjudications and the duty to help the distressed and oppressed; both duties remain and neither is destroyed by coming into conflict with the other.

We are prompted to theorise about morality partly because such conflicts notoriously arise. If a harmony of principles and dispositions seemed attainable, the problem of giving a rational reconstruction of acceptable moral judgments, and of their grounds, would seem directly soluble. But we know from direct experience that it is our nature to be pulled in contrary directions by the principles that are acceptable to us and in respect of the dispositions that we admire and that we wish to have.

The point could be put in another way. If our moral intuitions seemed to form a harmonious system of compatible claims, there would be a less radical difference between animals guided by instinct, in accordance with natural laws, towards their natural way of life and human beings guided by moral intuitions, which would also guide them towards the one way of life that has to be presumed to be natural to them. But we in fact find that a conflict of moral claims is natural to us, and that there are contrary dispositions that are immediately admirable and desirable. We not only find these conflicts in our unreflective intuitions and in commonplace morality; we may also find, after reflection on the source and nature of our moral intuitions, that these conflicts are unavoidable and not to be softened or glozed over. It seems an unavoidable feature of moral experience that men should be torn between the moral claims entailed by effectiveness in action, and particularly in politics, and the moral claims derived from the ideals of scrupulous honesty and integrity: between candour and kindness: between spontaneity and conscientious care: between open-mindedness, seeing both sides of a case, and loyalty to a cause. Such dispositions as these, and the contrary moral claims associated with them, generate the more difficult moral problems, because morality originally appears in our experience as a conflict of claims and a division of purpose.

An ideal of rationality is the instrument sometimes used to soften and to eliminate such conflicts as these; and this result is achieved by showing that the reasons that explain apparently conflicting moral claims form a coherent system and lead back to a common basis, to a single reason behind all moral claims. This was the argument of Plato's Republic, and the same theme is pursued by moral philosophers who are consequentialists, explaining away contrary moral claims as uncertainty about outcomes.

What is the force, and what is the consequence, of denying any ideal of rationality for practical reason that entails the softening or elimination of ultimate conflicts? Is there an *a priori* and general argument which corresponds to the argument from rationality and which shows that ineliminable conflicts among moral claims are to be expected by wise and truthful men, and not an ultimate harmony among moral claims? It is part of the force of the denial of harmony that no sufficient reason of any kind is on occasion available to explain a decision made after careful reflection in a situation of moral conflict; and that this lack of sufficient reason is not ground for apology, because our divided, and comparatively open, nature requires one to choose, without sufficient reason, between irreconcilable dispositions and contrary claims; there is unavoidably a breakdown of clear reasoning in choosing what the future is to be, because the reflective and second-order desires which, coupled with beliefs, guide the choices point to goals which are irreconcilable in the actual world and are harmonised only in an ideal world. That there should be a conflict between reflective desires, unreconciled outside an ideal world, is itself a condition of continuing moral development, both of the individual and of the species. If there is no valid theory to serve as the ground of a choice between irreconcilable dispositions, different choices will tend to be made by different men; and this vagary of choice will have an effect, being a form of experiment, in the development of the species. In the history of an individual the choices that he makes in conflicts between duties and reflective inclinations and purposes will constitute his own character as an individual. The causes explaining his choice will not all be found in rational assent to a valid theory. His imagination of possibilities has its part, and so do intuitions that he cannot fully explain, arising from experience.

7

Sometimes, and particularly often in politics and government, the decision in a situation of conflict involves a trade-off; for instance, a certain amount of liberty for the individual is traded-off in exchange for a clear general increase in welfare. Sufficient reason is on some occasions lacking in such decisions because there is still no compelling principle, or rational method, of balancing one value against another. But there is a more radical lack of sufficient reason in cases where it would be misleading to speak of a trade-off; this is where a conflict between different ways of life arises and where there is no way of achieving a reasonable and coherent compromise between them. The conflict is not between two values which in more fortunate circumstances could both be realised; but it is a conflict between two ways of life neither of which could ever be fully realised without some deliberate impairment of the other. Perhaps one could never in politics be entirely loyal and helpful to one's personal friends and entirely impartial and effective in serving the public interest; sooner or later there will in the common course of things be a conflict, as loyalty entails partiality. One could properly speak of a trade-off if one was trying to combine a decent degree of loyalty to friends with a decent degree of impartiality. The trade-off between antithetical values would then be the pursuit of an Aristotelian balance, an intuitive moral compromise that repudiates two extremes on either side. The Aristotelian balance between public and private life, with their attached virtues, and between practical and theoretical interests, is a feature of that particular way of life. The pressing moral problems within this way of life are problems of priorities, which can equally well be thought of as trade-offs; how do I balance the moral claims of friendship against the duties of public life? In a complete life a defensible order of priorities can be with luck achieved and with luck an overall balance realised; and this is the moral ideal within this way of life, the Aristotelian ideal.

There is a well known and radical type of conflict in which there is no trade-off and no compromise and no striking of a balance; a man has a mission, to which he is dedicated, which cannot now be fulfilled without his leaving his family behind, a desertion that will make them unhappy. He either goes or he stays, and there is no middle way. He has a yes-or-no choice, which can be represented as a choice between two moral claims, one of which will be taken to override the other; a choice also between two characters that may in future be imputed to him, as a man dedicated to his particular mission or as a man cherishing his family; a choice between two ways of life, both of which are represented by moral claims which he acknowledges. The yes-or-no decision also takes milder, familiar forms in the common run of experience; for instance, there is the recurring choice between telling the truth, where someone has a right to ask and to know, and not telling a truth which will cause pain. This may be approached by an Aristotelian moralist, dedicated to that way of life that has a just balance between dispositions as its ideal, as a matter of finding the right middle path in the particular circumstances: how much suffering, how great a deviation from truth, would be relevantly asked. But to a utilitarian dedicated to the avoidance and prevention of suffering, because his way of life has this ideal as its centre, one claim plainly overrides the other; and there have been men dedicated to truthfulness as a central ideal, who would find that this duty must always override the duty to avoid causing pain. There is a third possibility: that a man is divided, uncertain and hesitant between two ways of life, and also rejects the Aristotelian ideal of a just balance. At the centre of one way of life, which he has seen nobly realised, are ideals of entire truthfulness, integrity, strength of character: at the centre of another way of life, of which he has also seen an impressive example, is an ideal of gentleness and of a clear-headed concern for the actual feelings of others as having priority over everything else. So he is divided between the two moral claims in conflict, exactly as the man divided between his mission and his family, in the example mentioned earlier. For him there is an ultimate choice focussed on this occasion between two ways of life, and he cannot refer this conflict of moral claims to an order of priority among the virtues constituting his ideal way of life; nor can he ask himself which duty is of overriding importance within the way of life that he has already adopted as his own. He may invoke a number of religious or philosophical or historical beliefs in support of his choice; 'ultimate' does not mean the same as 'unargued' and 'unsupported'. But he has no recourse to already established beliefs of his which are also moral beliefs. The whole framework of moral belief has been called in question by this particular conflict.

Any actual choice between two ways of life, which comes to a head in a particular conflict of duties, arises from dense personal experience, and as a consequence of a man's particular conditions of life, and of his philosophical beliefs. No more can be said in general terms, except that morality does unalterably have this aspect of commitment to a way of life, even though many persons may never consciously confront such an ultimate choice. They are ready to recognise the possibility of an ultimate conflict. They are aware of an oppenness at the margin of morality and in their own way of life. There is some wilfulness, as well as naturalness, in the structure of practice and belief that they have accepted or imposed, and they recognise this, when they reflect. They know that they may be confronted with a conflict of duties which expresses a point of divergence between two ways of life, both of which have a nobility and worth, but which cannot under actual conditions be combined. The problem then has for them no rational solution. They will be guided by intuition, which entails reflecting on the two possibilities as fully as possible and then coming to a conclusion for reasons which they cannot arrange in a conclusive argument. A decision in an ultimate conflict may commit the agent to a way of life, which will extend in time indefinitely, as far as he knows, and, as far as he knows, it will close certain possibilities to him for ever, even though they are possibilities that he had thought of as being very highly desirable and valuable.

In private life, and outside politics, a one-sided commitment, the incurring of a very great cost in valuable activity renounced, sometimes seems an overriding requirement, just as sometimes the striking of a balance between conflicting claims sometimes seems an overriding moral requirement. There is no superior principle that is invoked in deciding between these two possibilities. To some men a narrow specialisation of achievement presents itself as an overriding moral requirement because of some outstanding value, perhaps of aesthetics or of science or religion, to which they are committed to the exclusion of all others; to others the neglect of competing moral claims, which the specialisation entails, is repugnant and seems inhuman, and they reject it as impossible from a moral point of view. That there should be both these irreconcilable opinions, and that one mind might not unreasonably oscillate between them, is expected in the common order of experience, and is familiar from episodes in history and in literature. The commitment may emerge from prolonged reflection and from a review of philosophical, religious, political and scientific beliefs; and yet the final intuitions of the right way, as it seems, may be very incompletely explained. Every reflective person has had the experience of oscillating between two possible descriptions of his own conduct, whether it is actual conduct or only envisaged conduct; one correct description makes the conduct acceptable and not to be despised, and the other correct description mentions features of the conduct which make it morally questionable and regrettable. Two competing ways of life, between which a man chooses, explicitly or implicitly, may impose different descriptions on the same envisaged conduct, which may emerge as prohibited in virtue of the descriptions relevant to one way of life and as positively required within another way of life. It is not only that the priorities to be aimed at are different in the two ways of life, both in respect of moral claims and of dispositions; but also the questions that one asks about a course of conduct, before evaluating it, will tend to be different.

8

It should now be possible to exhibit the principal differences between public morality and the morality of private life rather more clearly. In both spheres of practical thinking, which obviously overlap, 'abstract computational morality' properly has a pejorative sense, for the reasons given. The model of practical reasoning in difficult and substantial cases over-simplifies the difficulties by over-assimilation to reasoning in theoretical inquiries which demand coherence; it leaves too little place for intuitive discrimination alongside abstract general principles and the explicit computation of consequences. But the differences between public and private life have forced themselves on men's attention, and they enter into Machiavelli's perennial problem of the necessity of 'dirty hands' in great political and social enterprises. The evident elements of Machiavelli's problem can be listed:

(a) Public policy is a greater thing, as Aristotle remarked, and an agent in the public domain normally has responsibility for greater and more enduring consequences and consequences that change more men's lives.

(b) Violence, and the threat of violence or of force, have always been in prospect in public life and in the execution of public policies. In the normal run of things the moral problems associated with the use of force, and with war and violence, do not now arise in private life. The occasional use of violence, and the normal uses of force and of threats of force, introduce their own moral conflicts.

(c) In modern politics, and particularly in a democracy, one is reasonably required to protect the interests of those whom one in some sense represents, whether they be one's followers in a party or fellow citizens. There are obligations and duties specifically attached to representative roles.

Taking (a) and (c) together, the conclusion to be drawn is that there is an added responsibility in public affairs, and, secondly, this responsibility falls most heavily on the consequences of policies in the lives and fortunes of great numbers of persons unknown to those forming the policies. Machiavelli stressed this conclusion more vividly than any other writer ever has. He argued that it was irresponsible and morally wrong to apply to political action the moral standards that are appropriate to private life and to personal relations: standards of friendship and of justice. If one refused to be ruthless in pursuit of objectives in public policy, and refused to use deceit and guile as instruments of policy, one betrayed those who had put their trust in the man who represents them. Deceit and violence and the breaking of promises and undertakings are normal in the relations between states, and it seemed unlikely, in the sixteenth century, that they would cease to be normal. Public policies are rightly judged by their consequences, not by the intrinsic quality of the acts involved in their execution, which, when considered separately, are often unacceptable in the light of the moral standards of private life. Machiavelli implied that morality in politics must be a consequentialist morality, and the 'must' here marks a moral injunction. A fastidiousness about the means employed, appropriate in personal relations, is a moral dereliction in a politician, and the relevant moral criterion for a great national enterprise is lasting success; and success is measured by a historian's yardstick: continuing power, prosperity, high national spirit, a long-lasting dominance of the particular state or nation in the affairs of men. So Machiavelli argued. Below the level of state politics, any representative role or official position, which confers power, to some degree imposes a responsibility for the well-being of persons not directly known.

Professor Nagel in this volume examines ruthlessness and the bias to a consequentialist morality in politics, and I will not develop the point. There is a further ground of distinction between public and private morality: that there is a greater requirement of explicitness of reasoning in public morality than in private. Partly because of the bias towards a consequentialist criterion, and partly because of representative roles in politics, there is a requirement that an agent in politics should be able to give an account of the reasons for his policies, both as a defence of the policies that he is following and as an explanation of his following them. He normally needs an endorsement that his policies are right from his followers; and he needs to be understood by his followers, who will otherwise tend to distrust him if they do not know, or do not think that they know, how he thinks about substantial moral issues and what his calculations of consequences are. In summary, there is a requirement that his actions should fit together into explicitly formulated policies with more or less clearly specified consequences in view. When a policy is attacked, appeals to intuitions of right and wrong will usually not be an adequate defence. In private life such appeals often have a natural place in answering criticism, because it is recognised that the judgment required is not principally a judgment of calculable consequences, but of more complex and disparate values; and also of some values which do not involve calculation of consequences, in matters of love and friendship and fairness and integrity.

The moral infamies of the American intervention in Vietnam are not to be imputed to the fact that American policy-makers looked to the future, calculating consequences in resisting Communist expansion, but to the fact that their calculations were not tempered by respect for the ordinary moral decencies. The fault was not in the fact of calculation, but in the extreme crudity, the insensitiveness and lack of perception, the false definiteness and false clarity of the calculations. An illusory image of rationality distorted the moral judgment of the American policy-makers. They thought that their opponents in the U.S.A. were sentimental and guided only by their unreflective emotions, while they, the policy-makers, were computing consequences with precision and objectivity, using quasi-quantitative methods. They ignored, and remained insensitive to, the full nature and quality of their acts in waging the war, and of the shame and odium attached to some particular acts. They had the minimum of natural feeling for, and perception of, the peculiar mechanical brutality and unfeelingness of their conduct of the war, as it appeared to those who were not calculating so simply. The necessary blend between rational policy-making on the one side and natural feelings and reflective intuitions of right and wrong on the other had been distorted by a naive and mechanical Machiavellianism, which finally failed. The policy-makers were corrupted in judgment of consequences by the pseudo-rationalistic vocabulary in which they discussed 'options'. Under the influence of bad social science, and the bad moral philosophy that usually goes with it, they over-simplified the moral issues and provided an example of false rationality.

9

The public policies of any interest group or party normally have a theoretical background in a commonly professed set of moral beliefs. Specific policies need to be referred back to the set of moral beliefs which are held in common within the social or national group or party. A moral conflict, which expresses a division between two ways of life, is often a division of loyalties, and often entails more than an isolated individual choice; it often entails a political commitment.

I am not arguing that different moralities, in the sense of

different sets of prescriptions, are to be applied in private and in public life, as if these were self-contained spheres of activity. The claim is rather that the assumption of a political role, and of powers to change men's lives on a large scale, carry with them not only new responsibilities, but a new kind of responsibility, which entails, first, accountability to one's followers, secondly, policies that are to be justified principally by their eventual consequences, and, thirdly, a witholding of some of the scruples that in private life would prohibit one from using people as a means to an end and also from using force and deceit. The differences in these respects are matters of degree and of balance, but they are real differences. In addition to moral seriousness in justice and fairness to individuals, in love and friendship, constituting the sphere of private life, there is also political seriousness, seriousness in the use of power; and this requires higher priority for some duties and corresponding virtues and lower priority for refinements. In particular, it requires priority for duties of careful and responsible calculation, for the virtues of prudence and 'cleverness', cleverness being that Aristotelian component in moral virtue which political responsibility demands.

10

The three-tiered conception of morality outlined in 'Morality and Pessimism' (Chapter 1) is designed to make intelligible the complex relation of private and political morality. Conflict between competing ways of life – religious, ideological, national, family and class conflict – has been perpetual and conflict is always to be expected; and the conflicts are not only in the realm of ideas, but are often also political conflicts, involving force and the threat of force. A way of life is protected and maintained by the exercise of political power, and that way of life will evolve, and will change with changing forms of knowledge, as long as sufficient political protection of it lasts.

But one must not exaggerate the historical, time-dependent elements in admired and desired and sought after ways of life. There are evident uniformities in love and friendship and justice, and in the more pressing moral claims recognised in almost any known social organisation above the most primitive level. There is some constancy in the virtues almost universally recognised as essential in any person who is to be praised and respected as a person. The difference comes in the priorities among the virtues recognised in different ways of life, subject to different historical circumstances, and in the duties, rights and obligations consequently recognised, and in the priorities among these various moral claims.

II

Moral theory cannot be rounded off and made complete and tidy; partly because so much that is of value in a human life depends upon uncontrollable accident, partly because we still know so little about the determinants of behaviour and about human nature generally, partly because individuals vary so greatly in their dispositions and interests, partly because new ways of life should always be expected to arise in association with new knowledge and with new social forms. There is one further reason; we expect also leaps of the imagination, moments of insight, very rarely, and in unusual men, which will lead to transformations of experience and to new moral ambitions and to new enjoyments of living.

3 Politics and Moral Character

BERNARD WILLIAMS

What sorts of person do we want and need to be politicians? This question, and the broader question of what we morally want from politics, are importantly different from the question of what the correct answers are to moral problems which present themselves within political activity. We may want – we may *morally* want – politicians who on some occasions ignore those problems. Moreover, even in cases where what we want the politician to do is to consider, and give the right answer to, such a problem, it is not enough to say that we want him to be the sort of person who can do that. Since some of the correct answers involve actions which are nonetheless very disagreeable, further questions arise about the sorts of persons who will give – in particular, who may find it too easy to give – those right answers.

It is cases where the politician does something morally disagreeable, that I am concerned with: the problem that has been called that of *dirty hands*. The central question is: how are we to think about the involvement of politicians in such actions, and about the dispositions that such involvement requires? This is not in the first place a question about what is permissible and defensible in such connexions; though something, obviously, will have to be said about what it means to claim that a politician has adequate reason to do something which is, as I put it, 'morally disagreeable'.

The discussion assumes that it makes some difference what politicians are like, what dispositions they have. I do not want to stress an individualist picture of political action too much, but I assume that there is something to be said in the moral dimension about the actions of individual politicians. Even someone who denied that might admit, I suppose, that it could make some difference, of the sort which concerns us morally, what politicians were like. Someone who denies all that will probably think that morality has nothing to do with politics at all, and for him the whole area of discussion lapses.

It is widely believed that the practice of politics selects at least for cynicism and perhaps for brutality in its practitioners. This belief, and our whole subject, notoriously elicit an uncertain tone from academics, who tend to be either over-embarrassed or under-embarrassed by moralizing in the face of power. Excited, in either direction, by the subject, they often take rather large-scale or epic examples, such as the conduct of international relations by hostile powers, or ruthless policies which may or may not be justified by history. I will touch marginally on those kinds of issue at the end, but my first concern is more with the simply squalid end of the subject, and with the politician not so much as national leader or maker of history, but as professional. I shall defer the more heady question of politicians being criminals in favour of the more banal notion that they are crooks.

There is of course one totally banal sense of the claim that they are crooks, namely that some break the law for their own advantage, take bribes, do shady things which are not actually illegal for personal gain. This dimension of effort is for the purpose of the present discussion beside the point. It does raise one or two interesting questions, for instance the absence from politics of any very robust notion of professional ethics. Some professions, such as lawyers and doctors, have elaborate codes of professional ethics: I take it that this is not because their vocation rises nobly above any thoughts of personal gain, but because their clients need to be protected, and be seen to be protected, in what are particularly sensitive areas of their interests. Some areas of business have similar provisions, but in general the concept of a professional business ethic is less developed than that of a professional medical or legal ethic. One might think that politics was concerned quite generally with sensitive areas of the clients' interests, yet even in places where it is recognized that these restrictions govern the activities of doctors and lawyers, the politician's professional conduct is perceived as more like that of the business man. The explanation of this fact I take not to be very mysterious: roughly, there are several reasons why it is in the interest of most in these professions to belong to a respectable cartel, but in the case of politicians, the circumstances in which

they are able to run a cartel are circumstances in which they have
little motive to keep it respectable.

How are the morally dubious activities which belong to this,
irrelevant, class, distinguished from those which concern our
enquiry? Certainly not by the first sort being *secret*. For the first
sort are often not secret, and in some cultures are barely meant
to be so, it being an achievement calling for admiration that one
has stolen extensively and conspicuously from the public funds.
Even more obviously, many dubious acts of the more strictly
political kind are themselves secret. The point rather is that not
all acts done by politicians are political acts, and we are concerned
with those that are. Relative to some appropriate account of what
the politician is supposed to be up to as a politician, stealing from
public funds is likely to count as a diversion of effort. However,
it is to be recognized that not all classifications which would be
made on these principles by the most respectable north-west
European or North American opinion would come out the same
elsewhere; thus bribery can be an integral and functional part of
a political system. What must count as a political activity any-
where, however, is *trying to stay in office*. There are, needless to
say, unacceptable ways of staying in office, and there are among
them ways of staying in office which defeat the purposes of the
methods for acquiring office (rigging the ballot). But this is a
matter of means – the *objective* of staying in office, though it cannot
by every means or in every circumstance be decently attained, is
itself highly relevant to the business of politics, whereas the
objectives of enriching oneself or of securing sinecures for one's
family are not.

We shall leave aside the dubious activities of politicians which
are not primarily political activities. But since the question we shall
be concerned with is primarily what dispositions we want in
politicians, we should not at the same time forget the platitude
that the psychological distance between the two sorts of activity
may be very small indeed. Not every politically ruthless or devious
ruler is disposed to enrich himself or improperly advance his
friends: the ones who are not are usually morally and psychologically more interesting. But the two sorts of tendency go together
often enough, and cries for 'clean government' are usually demands for the suppression of both.

There is another aspect of the subject that I shall mention only in passing. I shall consider the politician as the originator of action, or at least as a joint originator of action, rather than as one who participates in a party or government, or acquiesces, with respect to decisions which he does not help to make. Some of the issues we shall consider apply to those who originate at any level; other larger issues apply only to those who originate at some higher level, such as a President or Prime Minister or (in the British system) a Cabinet Minister. This emphasis leaves on one side the question of a politician's responsibility, and hence the view one should take of him, when he agrees with a measure but did not originate it. It also leaves aside the more interesting question of his responsibility when he does not agree with it but acquiesces in it or stays in a position where he is identified with it – what is, in a democratic system at least, the *resigning problem*.

One remark is perhaps worth making here in relation to that problem. Resigning, or again refraining from resigning, cannot be straightforwardly either instrumental or expressive acts. Instrumental considerations of course bear on the issue, as in the classical 'working from within' argument which has kept many queasy people tied to many appalling ventures for remarkably long periods. Yet such decisions cannot, in the nature of the case, be purely and in all cases instrumental, since the decision has a class of consequences which themselves depend on the agent's being perceived as not being entirely consequentialist about it. Among the consequences of the act are some that depend on what it is taken to mean, so that the purely consequentialist agent would be faced, if he fully considered the consequences, with the fact that what he is doing is by its nature something which cannot be adequately thought about purely in terms of its consequences. On the other hand, to view resignation as the mere equivalent of saying ' I agree ' or ' I disagree ' in a private and uncoerced conversation would be an elementary misunderstanding, entertained only by someone who neglected the difference between a commitment to ongoing political activity, and a one-off example of political expression. It is also, therefore, to neglect the point that for a politician such a decision is, in a substantial and relevant sense, part of his life.

When that point is seen, moreover, it is often seen in the wrong terms: it naturally invites being seen in the wrong terms. For a career politician, resignation is likely to affect the relation of his life to politics altogether. He must consider the decision to resign in the context of a commitment to a political life, and that can of course be read as his attending to his career. No doubt it is true of some in this situation that they are simply attending to their career, but it is important, both for the public and for the politician, to recognize that there is a structural reason why it should be difficult to tell whether that is true or not.

Among political acts are some for which there are good political reasons, as that important and worthy political projects would fail without these acts, but which are acts which honourable, scrupulous etc. people might, *prima facie* at least, be disinclined to do. Besides those, there are more, and more insidious, cases in which the unpalatable act seems necessary not to achieve any such clear-cut and noble objective, but just to keep going, or to pre-empt opposition to a worthy project, or more generally to prevent a worthy project becoming impossible later. What the unpalatable acts may be depends on the political environment; at present we are concerned with a relatively ordered situation where political activity involves at least bargaining and the expression of conflicting interests and ideals. In such a situation a politician might find himself involved in, or invited to, such things as: lying, or at least concealment and the making of misleading statements; breaking promises; special pleading; temporary coalition with the distasteful; sacrifice of the interests of worthy persons to those of unworthy persons; and (at least if in a sufficiently important position) coercion up to blackmail. We are not at this point considering more drastic situations in which there is a question, for instance, of having opponents killed. (I mean by that, that *there is no question of it*, and it would be thought outrageous or insane to mention it as an option. The situation is not one of those in which such options are mentioned and then, all things considered, laid aside.)

The less drastic, but still morally distasteful, activities are in no way confined to politics. That they should seem necessary follows just from there being large interests involved, in a context of partly unstructured bargaining. It is the same, for instance, with a lot of business of the more active variety. But it attracts more obloquy in politics than elsewhere: the use of such means is thought more appropriate to the pursuit of professedly self-interested ends than where larger moral pretensions are entertained. But the fact that there are larger moral pretensions is itself not an accident. Besides the point that some objectives other than the self-interest of the professional participants are necessary – at the limit, are necessary for the activity even to be politics – there is the point that democracy has a tendency to impose higher expectations with regard even to the means, since under democracy control of politicians is precisely supposed to be a function of the expectations of the electorate.

I have mentioned acts, done in pursuit of worthy political ends, which 'honourable, scrupulous etc. people might, *prima facie* at least, be disinclined to do'. But, it will be said, if it is for some worthy political objective and the greater good, does not that merely show that it is an act which these honourable people should *not* be disinclined to do? At most, the characteristic which the act possesses is that it is of a type which these people would be disinclined to do if it were not in this interest; and that, it may be said, is irrelevant. But this Utilitarian response either does not get to the question which concerns us, or else gives an inadequate answer to it. It does not get to the question if it merely insists that the otherwise discreditable act is the one, in these circumstances, to be done, and says nothing about the dispositions of the agent, and how his dispositions express themselves in a view of this act. It gives an inadequate answer if it says that the only disposition such an agent needs is the disposition to do what is Utilitarianly right. Even Utilitarians have found that answer inadequate: it is not self-evident, and many Utilitarians agree that it is not even true, that the best way to secure their objective of the greatest happiness all round is to have agents each of whom is pursuing, as such, the greatest happiness all round. Beyond that level of discussion, again, there is the deeper point that moral dispositions other than Utilitarian benevolence may themselves figure in people's conceptions of 'happiness'.

In any case, it is not enough to say that these are situations in which the right thing to do is an act which would *normally* be morally objectionable. That description best fits the case in which an act and its situation constitute an *exception*. We may recall the repertoire, familiar from Ross and other writers, of obligations properly overridden in emergencies. There, the decision is often easy – of course we break the routine promise to save the drowning child, and to doubt it, or to feel uneasy about having done it, would be utterly unreasonable. It is a clear overriding circumstance. While it is not as though the promise or other defeated obligation had never existed (one still has the obligation at least to explain), nevertheless it is quite clearly and unanswerably overridden, and complaints from the disadvantaged party would, once things had been explained, be unacceptable. Of course, not all cases of the straight overriding kind are clear cases of that kind. One can be in doubt what to do, and here there is room for unease. But the unease, within this structure, is directly related to the doubt or unclarity: the question will be 'did I really do the right thing?'. If one has an uneasy sense that one may have done wrong to the victim, it is because one has an uneasy sense that one may have done the wrong thing.

Some situations in politics are no doubt of that structure. But the situations I have in mind (of course, as I have said, they are not confined to politics) are of a different structure. In these, the sense that a discreditable thing has been done is not the product of uncertainty, nor again of a recognition that one has made the wrong choice. A sense that something discreditable has been done will, moreover, be properly shared by the victims, and they will have a complaint that they have been wronged. The politician who just could not see that they had a complaint, and who, after he had explained the situation to them, genuinely thought that their complaint was based on a misunderstanding and that they were unreasonable to make it (as one might properly think in the first kind of case) is a politician whose dispositions are already such as to raise our questions in a very pressing form.

I do not have in mind here drastic cases of tragic choice, where one might say that whatever the agent did was wrong.[1] They, though not merely exceptions, are certainly exceptional. The cases we are considering are not just what our normal categories count as exceptions, nor are they of the exceptional kind that reaches beyond our normal categories. Nor, again, need the decision be at all uncertain. It will often be true of these cases that so long

---

[1] I have said something about such cases in 'Ethical Consistency', reprinted in *Problems of the Self* (Cambridge 1973), Ch. 11.

as the agent takes seriously the moral frames of reference or reasons which support each of the courses of action, it will not be unclear what he should do. But the clarity in such a case is not that of the vivid emergency exception; nor is it the clarity of the impossible, which can attend the tragic case. It is clear because it is everyday, part of the business: not too often part of the business, one hopes, but part of the business all the same. If the politician is going to take the claims of politics seriously, including the moral claims of politics, and if he is going to act at anything except a modest and largely administrative level of responsibility, then he has to face at least the probability of situations of this kind. If he shares the highest responsibilities, it is virtually certain that he will encounter them. Below that level, he may perhaps not. He may operate in a very docile and citizenly environment. He may be lucky. He may even have, as a few seem to have, a virtue or a moral cunning which drives such situations away. But it is a predictable and probable hazard of public life that there will be these situations in which something morally disagreeable is clearly required. To refuse on moral grounds ever to do anything of that sort is more than likely to mean that one cannot seriously pursue even the moral ends of politics.

Yet, at the same time, the moral disagreeableness of these acts is not merely cancelled, and this comes out above all in the consideration that the victims can justly complain that they have been wronged. It is undeniable, for instance, that the agent has lied, or deliberately misled them, or bullied them, or let them down, or used them. It may be that when it is all explained, they understand, but it is foolish to say, even then, that they have no right to complain.

It may be said that the victims do not have a right to complain because their relation to the action is not the same in the political context as it would be outside it: perhaps it is not even the same action. There is some truth, sometimes, in this claim. It does apply to some victims themselves involved in politics: a certain level of roughness is to be expected by anyone who understands the nature of the activity, and it is merely a misunderstanding to go on about it in a way which might be appropriate to more sheltered activities. But this consideration – which might be called *Truman's kitchen-heat principle* – does not go all the way. There are victims outside politics, and there are victims inside it who get worse than they could reasonably expect; and in general there are political acts which no considerations about appropriate expectations or the going currency of the trade can in themselves adequately excuse.

I mentioned the 'moral claims' of politics. In some cases, the claims of the political reasons are proximate enough, and enough of the moral kind, to enable one to say that there is a moral justification for that particular political act, a justification which has outweighed the moral reasons against it. Even so, that can still leave the moral remainder, the uncancelled moral disagreeableness I have referred to. The possibility of such a remainder is not peculiar to political action, but there are features of politics which make it specially liable to produce it. It particularly arises in cases where the moral justification of the action is of a consequentialist or maximizing kind, while what has gone to the wall is a right: there is a larger moral cost attached to letting a right be overridden by consequences, than to letting one consequence be overridden by another, since it is part of the point of rights that they cannot just[2] be overridden by consequences. In politics the justifying consideration will characteristically be of the consequentialist kind. Moreover, an important aspect of consequentialist reasoning lies in maximizing *expectation*, the product of the size of the pay-off and its probability. Since in the political sphere of action the pay-offs are, or can readily be thought to be, very large, the probabilities can be quite small, and the victims may find that their rights have been violated for the sake of an outside chance.

Where the political reasons are of the less proximate kind, for instance defensive, or pre-emptive, or concerned with securing an opportunity, we may speak, not of the moral claims of politics, but merely of the claims of politics against morality. While an anxious politician may hope still to find some moral considerations bearing on the situation, he may discover that they have retreated merely to the overall justification of the pursuit of his, or his party's, worthwhile objectives, or some similar over-arching con-

---

[2] I assume that rights can sometimes be overridden. To define 'rights' so that this should not ever be possible would have wider consequences – since one must say something about possible conflicts of rights among themselves – and is anyway undesirable: if all rights have to be *absolute* rights, then it is plausible to conclude that there are no rights at all.

cern. The Olympian point of retreat is notoriously so distant and invulnerable that the rationale of seriously[3] carrying on the business of politics ceases to be disturbed by any moral qualms or any sense of non-political costs at all. Decent political existence lies somewhere between that – or its totally cynical successor, from which even the distant view of Olympus has disappeared – and an absurd failure to recognize that if politics is to exist as an activity at all, some moral considerations must be expected to get out of its way.

If that space is to have any hope of being occupied, we need to hold on to the idea, and to find some politicians who will hold on to the idea, that there are actions which remain morally disagreeable even when politically justified. The point of this is not at all that it is edifying to have politicians who, while as ruthless in action as others, are unhappy about it. Sackcloth is not suitable dress for politicians, least of all successful ones. The point – and this is basic to my argument – is that only those who are reluctant or disinclined to do the morally disagreeable when it is really necessary have much chance of not doing it when it is not necessary.

There are two different reasons for this. First, there is no disposition which just consists in getting it right every time, whether in politics or in anything else. Whether judgment is well exercised, whether immediate moral objections are given the right weight, or any, against large long-term issues, is, on any sensible view of those processes, something that involves patterns of senti-ment and reaction. In a body of persons considering a practical question, it essentially involves their shared dispositions and their mutual expectations – what considerations can be heard, what kinds of hesitation or qualification or obstacle it is appropriate or effective to mention. (There is a remark attributed to Keynes, about an American official: 'a man who has his ear so close to the ground that he cannot hear what an upright man says'.) That is the first, and main, reason, and one which any reasonable view of deliberation must accept: a habit of reluctance is an essential obstacle against the happy acceptance of the intolerable.

[3] I have known a politician, now dead, who used to say 'that is not a *serious* political argument' to mean, more or less, 'that is an argument about what to do in politics which mentions a non-political consideration' – in particular, a moral consideration. This posture was to some degree bluff.

The second reason, which I have already included in my account, is something less widely acceptable: that reluctance in the necessary case, is not only a useful habit, but a correct reaction *to that case*, because that case does involve a genuine moral cost. The fact that reluctance is justified even in the necessary case – and in speaking of 'reluctance', I mean not just initial hesitation in reaching for the answer, but genuine disquiet when one arrives at it – is in fact something that helps to explain the nature, and the value, of the habit of reluctance which was appealed to in the first reason. It embodies a sensibility to moral costs. Utilitarianism, which hopes (in some of its indirect forms) to appeal to habits of reluctance, cannot in fact make any sense of them at this level, because it lacks any sense of *moral* cost, as opposed to costs of some other kind (such as utility) which have to be considered in arriving at the moral decision. Utilitarianism has its special reasons for not understanding the notion of a moral cost, which are connected with its maximizing conceptions; but much other moral philosophy shares that incapacity. Yet it is a notion deeply entrenched in many people's moral consciousness. Why so many moral philosophers learn to forget it is a harder question, and perhaps a deeper one, than why some politicians do.

If, then, there can be agents who in this way have good moral reason to do things which they have good reason to think are, and remain, morally distasteful, a way of understanding their situation might be to see it as one in which the agent has some special relationship to parties involved, which will give him an honourable motive for overruling his objections to such acts. This is the model which Charles Fried in a recent paper ('The Lawyer as Friend: The Moral Foundations of the Lawyer–Client Relation', 85 *Yale Law Journal*, 1060–89 (1976)) has applied to the case (in some ways similar) of the lawyer who is required on behalf of his client to do things one would not feel morally well-disposed towards doing, such as harassing witnesses or pressing a formal advantage of well-off persons against the vital interests of less well-off persons. Fried invokes in this connexion the relationship of friendship, modelling the lawyer's relationship to his client on the kind of personal relationship which would be widely acknowledged to permit or even require departures from what would otherwise be the demands of impartiality. Fried honestly raises and confronts the problem, but it is hard to be convinced by the model that he has brought to bear on it. For one thing – a point which he mentions but, it seems to me, does not dispose of – one is not paid to be someone's friend; for another, the honourable man who is in question might not be expected to have friends who are like some of the lawyer's clients, or who expect him to do what some of the lawyer's clients expect him to do.

There are some analogies to a special relationship model in politics, inasmuch as politics involves loyalties or allegiances which require one to be something other than impartial. But while there are some allegiances of this kind, to country or party or electorate, and they play some role, they are not adequate, any more than a personal relationship to the client in the legal case, to cover the full range of these issues. Rather, the legal case very readily presses on us a different sort of question which is not only a useful question to ask but also, I think, *the* useful question to ask in these connexions: namely, what sort of system does one want, and what sort of disposition do you want in the person acting? We then have to think about how the answers to these questions can be harmonized, in the light of the question: what dispositions does the system require or favour?

The example of the law raises some interesting questions in this connexion, and I shall pursue it a little further. One has to ask how the desired product of legal activity, justice, is related to an adversarial system, and to what extent the sorts of behaviour that concern Fried are encouraged or required by such a system. That is, in fact, only the start of the problem, for if the adversarial system succeeds in producing justice, one factor in that must be the presence of a judge – and judges are lawyers, and usually former advocates. The judicial disposition is not the same as the adversarial disposition, but as our system of recruitment for judges works, the one has somehow to issue from the other.

Let us, however, stick to the adversarial case. Concentrating on the morally disagreeable activities which may be involved in the enforcement of some legal rights (e.g. some legal rights of the strong against the weak), we might be tempted by the following argument:

(1) In any complex society (at least) the enforcement of some legal rights involves morally disagreeable acts.

(2) It is bad that legal rights which exist should not be enforceable.

(3) Enforcement of many rights of the kind mentioned in (1) requires lawyers.

(4) Any lawyer really effective in enforcing those rights must be fairly horrible.

ERGO (5) It is good that some lawyers are fairly horrible.

How might this argument be met, if at all? The conventional answer presumably lies in denying (1); but in our context of discussion, we will not accept as sufficient the conventional reason for denying it, namely that there is a sufficient moral justification for the system that requires those acts (which is in effect equivalent to (2)). Another line would be to deny (2). This is perhaps the approach of Wasserstrom,[4] who inclines to the view that if (1) carries much weight with regard to some rights, then it may just be better that those rights be not enforced. If this goes beyond the position of refusing to act when one knows that someone else will (not necessarily an objectionable position), it runs into difficulties about the operation of the law as a roughly predictable system. Fried denies (4), by putting the acts required in (1) into the framework of loyalty and friendship. Others might combat (4) by using notions of professionalism, insisting that since those acts are done in a professional role, in the name of a desirable system, it cannot follow that they express a horrible disposition – they are not, in that sense, personal acts at all.

The phenomenology of the states of mind invoked by that answer is very complex. The limitations of the answer are, however, fairly obvious and indeed notorious. One limitation, for instance, must lie in the consideration that it is a personal fact about somebody that that is his profession. However, whatever we think in general about those ideas of professionalism, there is at least one thing that can be allowed to the lawyer's situation which it is hard to allow to the politician's. Even if we accepted (5), the disagreeable conclusion of the argument, we could at least agree that the professional activities of lawyers are delimited enough to

[4] 'Lawyers as Professionals: some moral issues', 5 *Human Rights* (1975) pp. 2–24. I am grateful for discussion of these issues to Dick Wasserstrom, Andy Kaufman, and other participants in the Council for Philosophical Studies Institute on Law and Ethics, Williams College Mass., 1977.

make the fact that some are fairly horrible of limited account to
the public: the ways in which the argument, if sound, shows them
to be horrible are ways which their clients, at any rate, have no
reason to regret. But there is much less reason for such comfort
in the politicians' case, and if a comparable argument can be
mounted with them, then the public has reason to be alarmed.
The professional sphere of activity is very much less delimited,
and there are important asymmetries, for example in the matter
of concealment. The line between the client and the other side
is one which in an adversarial system governs a great deal of the
lawyer's behaviour, and certainly the sorts of reasons he has for
concealing things from the opposition are not characteristically
reasons for concealment from his client. But the reasons there are
for concealing things in politics are always reasons for concealing
them from the electorate.

Another reason for concern in the political case lies in the
professional (and in itself perfectly proper) commitment to staying
in power. I have already suggested that it involves an essential
ambivalence: it is impossible to tell, at the limit, where it merges
into simple ambition, and into that particular deformation of
political life, under all systems, which consists in the inability to
consider a question on its merits because one's attention is directed
to the consequences of giving (to one's colleagues, in the first
instance) a particular answer. Where that has widely taken over,
the citizens have reason to fear their politicians' judgment.

The dispositions of politicians are differently related to their
tasks and to their public than are those of a profession such as the
legal profession for which partly analogous questions arise. Those
differences all give greater reason for concern, and make more
pressing the question: what features of the political system are
likely to select for those dispositions in politicians which are at once
morally welcome and compatible with their being effective
politicians? What features of the system can help to bring it about
that fairly decent people can dispose of a fair degree of power?
How does one ensure a reasonable succession of colonists of the
space between cynicism and political idiocy?

It is a vast, old, and in good part empirical question. If one
adapts Plato's question, *how can the good rule?*, to Machiavelli's,
how to rule the world as it is?, the simplest conflation – *how can the*

good rule the world as it is? – is merely discouraging. It is also, however, excessively pious: the conception of the good that it inherits from Plato invites the question of how the good could do anything at all, while the Machiavellian conception of the world as it is raises the question of how anyone could do anything with it. (A popular sense of 'realism' gets its strength from the fact that the second of those questions has some answers, while the first has none.) But if one modifies from both ends, allowing both that the good need not be as pure as all that, so long as they retain some active sense of moral costs and moral limits; and that the society has some genuinely settled politics and some expectations of civic respectability: then there is some place for discussing what properties we should like the system, in these respects, to have. There are many: I will mention, only in barest outline, four dimensions of a political system which seem to bear closely on this issue.

(a) There is the question, already touched on, of the balance of publicity, and the relations of politician and public, particularly of course in a democracy. The assumption is widespread, particularly in the USA, that public government and a great deal of public scrutiny must encourage honest government, and apply controls to the cynicism of politicians. There is, however, no reason to suppose that the influence of such practices and institutions will be uniformly in one direction. The requirements of instant publicity in a context which is, as we are supposing, to some mild degree moralized, has an evident potential for hypocrisy, while, even apart from that, the instant identification of particular political acts, as they are represented at the degree of resolution achievable in the media, is a recipe for competition in pre-emptive press releases.

(b) A similar question is that of the relations of politicians to one another; and there is another approved belief, that it is in the interest of good government that politicians should basically be related to one another only functionally, that they should not share a set of understandings which too markedly differentiate them from people who are not politicians. Yet it is not clear how far this is true, either. For it is an important function of the relations of politicians to one another, what courses of action are even discussible, and that is a basic dimension of a moral culture. Very obviously, a ruthless clique is worse than a clique checked by less ruthless outsiders, but that is not the only option. Another is that of a less ruthless clique resisting more ruthless outsiders.

(c) A very well-known point is that of the relation of potential politicians to actual ones, the question of political recruitment. Notoriously, systems where succession is problematic or discontinuous have the property of selecting for the ruthless. No sensible critic will suggest that if that is so, it is at all easy to change, but it is nevertheless an important dimension of assessment of a political system.

(d) A slightly less obvious variant of the same sort of issue concerns the promotion-pattern within a political organization: in particular, the position of the bottleneck between very top jobs and rather less top jobs. Except in very favoured circumstances, it is likely to be the case that getting to the top of a political system will require properties which, while they need not at all necessarily be spectacularly undesirable or even regrettable, may nevertheless perhaps lean in the direction of the kind of ambition and professionalism which does not always make for the best judgment, moral or practical. It is desirable that the system should not put too heavy stress on those properties too soon in the business; there can then be an honourable and successful role, below the final bottleneck, for persons without the elbow-power to get into or through the bottleneck. Government concentrated on a few personalities of course tends to weaken this possibility. Related is the question of the prestige of jobs below the top one. It was a notable fact, remarked by some commentators, that when the English politician R. A. (now Lord) Butler retired from politics, it was suggested that his career had been a failure because – and although – he had held almost every major office of state except the Premiership itself.

These are, of course, only hints at certain dimensions of discussion. The aim is just to suggest that it is in such ways that one should think about the disagreeable acts involved in (everyday) politics – that fruitful thought should be directed to the aspects of a political system which may make it less likely that the only persons attracted to a profession which undoubtedly involves some such acts will be persons who are insufficiently disposed to find them disagreeable.

Last, I should like to make just one point about the further dimension of the subject, in which one is concerned not just with the disagreeable or distasteful but with crimes, or what otherwise would be crimes. This is a different level from the last: here we are concerned not just with business but, so to speak, with the Mafia. My question, rather as before, is not directly whether actions of a certain kind – in this case such things as murders, torture, etc. – are ever justified, but rather, if they are justified, how we should think of those who politically bring them about. I shall call the actions in question, for short, *violence*. It might be worth distinguishing, among official acts of violence, what could be called *structured* and *unstructured* violence: the former related to such processes as executions under law, application of legal force by the police, etc., while the latter include acts (it may be, more abroad than at home) pursued in what is regarded as the national interest.

I shall set out a list of four propositions which some would regard as all true, and which, if they were all true, would make the hope of finding politicians of honourable character, except in minor roles and in favourable circumstances, very slim.

(i) There are violent acts which the state is justified in doing which no private citizen as such would be justified in doing.

(ii) Anything the state is justified in doing, some official such as, often, a politician is justified in ordering to be done.

(iii) You are not morally justified in ordering to be done anything which you would not be prepared to do yourself.

(iv) Official violence is enough like unofficial violence for the preparedness referred to in (iii) to amount to a criminal tendency.

I take it that no-one except anarchists will deny (i), at least so far as structured violence is concerned (it is admitted that the distinction between structured and unstructured violence is imprecise). It may be said that structured violence constitutes acts which none but the state could even logically perform: thus nothing done by a private citizen as such could constitute a judicial execution. But I take it that while this is true, it does not cut very deep into the essential issues: thus there is another description of the act which is a judicial execution under which that act could logically, but ought not to be, performed by a private citizen. A more substantial issue is whether the only violence that is legitimate for the state is structured violence. This I doubt, too. Even if regular military operations are counted as structured violence, there may be other acts, bordering on the military or of an irregular character, which a state may be lucky if it is in a position to do without altogether.

An important issue connected with this is the extent to which a political leader's task, particularly in a democracy, is defined in terms of defending the interests of the state; and whether, if the interests of some other, rival, state will be advanced unless some act of violence is authorized, he can be justified in refusing to authorize that act. A similar problem arises in the case where he thinks that the interests of another state should, in justice, prevail. He certainly has a right to that opinion; to what extent has he the right to act on it while still performing that role?

The (imprecise) distinction between structured and unstructured violence also bears on (iv). (iv) is perhaps more plausible with unstructured than with structured violence. It is very widely agreed that the distinction between the official and the unofficial can make a moral difference to the estimation of acts of violence; there are similarly psychological differences in the dispositions underlying the two kinds of acts, even if it is unclear how deep those differences may, in many cases, go (an unclarity which itself makes some people unduly nervous about the legitimacy of official violence). If that is right, then (iv) will fail, and the disobliging conclusion will not follow from the argument, even granted the truth of (i) and the platitudinous truth of (ii). At least, it will be enough to prevent its following with full generality. But while we may certainly agree that (iv) is not exceptionlessly true, it is quite plausible to claim that there are acts, particularly perhaps of unstructured violence, for which (iv) really does hold true, but which nevertheless would be justified under (i). To suppose that there could be no such acts, to suppose in particular that if an act is such that (iv) applies to it, then it must follow that it could not be justified, would be, it seems to me, to take a highly unrealistic view either of politics, or of the possible psychology of agents who will do that act.

In this case, attention turns to (iii); (iii) seems to me false, and more interestingly so than (iv). If so, then there is perhaps a larger class of arguments which have some currency in moral discussion which will have to be abandoned or given extra help: as that one should be a vegetarian unless one would be prepared to work in an abattoir, or that one should not accept experimentation on animals unless one were prepared to conduct it (assuming that one had the skills) oneself. However it may be with those cases, at any rate our understanding of honesty and decency in politicians should be modified by reflexion on (iii). The consideration that they should not order something unless they were prepared to do it themselves should be counterweighted with the consideration that if they were prepared to do it themselves, they might be far too willing to order it.

4 Ruthlessness in Public Life

THOMAS NAGEL

I

The great modern crimes are public crimes. To a degree the same can be said of the past, but the growth of political power has introduced a scale of massacre and despoliation that makes the efforts of private criminals, pirates, and bandits seem truly modest.

Public crimes are committed by individuals who play roles in political, military, and economic institutions. (Because religions are politically weak, crimes committed on their behalf are now rare.) Yet unless the offender has the originality of Hitler, Stalin, or Amin, the crimes don't seem to be fully attributable to the individual himself. Famous political monsters have moral personalities large enough to transcend the boundaries of their public roles; they take on the full weight of their deeds as personal moral property. But they are exceptional. Not only are ordinary soldiers, executioners, secret policemen, and bombardiers morally encapsulated in their roles, but so are most secretaries of defense or state, and even many presidents and prime ministers. They act as office-holders or functionaries, and thereby as individuals they are insulated in a puzzling way from what they do: insulated both in their own view and in the view of most observers. Even if one is in no doubt about the merits of the acts in question, the agents seem to have a slippery moral surface, produced by their roles or offices.

This is certainly true of several American statesmen responsible for the more murderous aspects of policy during the Vietnam war. Robert McNamara is president of the World Bank. McGeorge Bundy is president of the Ford Foundation. Elliot Richardson was secretary of defense under Nixon during the completely illegal bombing of Cambodia which went on *after* the Vietnam peace agreements were signed. He then became attorney general and was

widely acclaimed for resigning that office rather than comply with
Nixon's request that he fire Archibald Cox for demanding the
White House tapes. His highly selective sense of honor has served
him well: he has since been ambassador to Britain, secretary of
commerce and ambassador at large, and we shall hear more of him.
Kissinger is of course a highly esteemed figure, despite the
Christmas bombing of 1972 and all that preceded it.

The judgments I am presupposing are controversial: not everyone agrees that American policy during the Vietnam war was
criminal. But even those who do think so may find it hard to attach
the crimes to the criminals, in virtue of the official role in which
they were committed. Few old anti-war demonstrators would feel
more than mildly uncomfortable about meeting one of these
distinguished figures, unless it was just because we were un-
accustomed to personal contact with anyone as powerful as the
president of the World Bank.

There is, I think, a problem about the moral effects of public
roles and offices. Certainly they have a profound effect on the
behavior of the individuals who fill them, an effect partly restrictive
but significantly liberating. Sometimes they confer great power,
but even where they do not, as in the case of an infantryman or
police interrogator, they can produce a feeling of moral insulation
that has strong attractions. The combination of special requirements and release from some of the usual restrictions, the ability
to say that one is only following orders or doing one's job or
meeting one's responsibilities, the sense that one is the agent of
vast impersonal forces or the servant of institutions larger than any
individual – all these ideas form a heady and sometimes corrupting
brew.

But this would not be so unless there were something to the
special status of action in a role. If roles encourage illegitimate
release from moral restraints it is because their moral effect has
been distorted. It will help to understand the distortion if we
consider another curiosity of current moral discourse about public
life: the emphasis placed on those personal restrictions that com-
plement the lack of official restraint – the other side of the coin of
public responsibility and irresponsibility. Public figures are not
supposed to use their power openly to enrich themselves and their
families, or to obtain sexual favors. Such primitive indulgences

are generally hidden or denied, and stress is laid on the personal probity and disinterest of public figures. This kind of personal detachment in the exercise of official functions is thought to guarantee their good moral standing, and it leaves them remarkably free in the public arena. No doubt private transgressions are widespread, but when they are inescapably exposed the penalty can be severe, for a delicate boundary of moral restraint that sets off the great body of public power and freedom has been breached. Spiro Agnew will never be head of the Ford Foundation.

The exchange seems fairly straightforward. The exercise of public power is to be liberated from certain constraints by the imposition of others, which are primarily personal. Because the office is supposedly shielded from the personal interests of the one who fills it, what he does in his official capacity seems also to be depersonalized. This nourishes the illusion that personal morality does not apply to it with any force, and that it cannot be strictly assigned to his moral account. The office he occupies gets between him and his depersonalized acts.

Among other things, such a picture disguises the fact that the exercise of power, in whatever role, is one of the most personal forms of individual self-expression, and a rich source of purely personal pleasure. The pleasure of power is not easily acknowledged, but it is one of the most primitive human feelings – probably one with infantile roots. Those who have had it for years sometimes realize its importance only when they have to retire. Despite their grave demeanor, impersonal diction, and limited physical expression, holders of public power are personally involved to an intense degree and probably enjoying it immensely. But whether or not it is consciously enjoyed, the exercise of power is a primary form of individual expression, not diminished but enhanced by the institutions and offices on which it depends.

When we try, therefore, to say what is morally special about public roles and public action, we must concentrate on how they alter the demands on the individual. The actions are his, whether they consist of planning to obliterate a city or only firing in response to an order. So if the moral situation is different from the case where he acts in no official capacity, it must be because the requirements are different.

II

It is hard to discuss this subject in general terms, since roles and offices differ so widely. Nevertheless, the question of the nature of the discontinuity between individual morality and public morality is in part a general one, because the answer must take one of two forms. Either public morality will be derivable from individual morality or it will not. The answer will vary greatly in detail from case to case, but if a significant element of public morality is not derivable from the moral requirements that apply to private individuals, it is probably a common feature of many different examples.

To give the question content, it is necessary to say more about derivability. The interesting question is whether the special features of public morality can be explained in terms of principles already present at the individual level, which yield apparent moral discontinuities when applied to the special circumstances of public life. If so, then public morality is in a substantive and not merely trivial sense derivable from private morality.[1] It emerges naturally from individual morality under the conditions that define the individual's public role.

This could still yield different moral requirements in two ways. Either the general principles could imply additional constraints on public action; or the principles could be such that certain requirements would cease to apply once one assumed a public role, because the conditions for their application would have disappeared. Or the change might involve some combination of the two. In view of the second kind of change, even if public morality is derivable from private, it is possible that the moral restraints on public action are weaker than those on individual action.

The alternative to derivability is that public morality is not grounded on individual morality, and that therefore people acting in certain official roles or capacities are required or permitted to do things that cannot be accounted for on that basis. This also

---

[1] Public morality becomes trivially derivable from individual morality if individual morality is extended to include all true propositions of the form, 'if the individual is acting in public role X, he may (or must) do Y', and so forth. This is compatible, however, with there being no connection between the grounds of the public and private requirements.

might take two forms. They might come under restrictions in areas left free by individual morality: public officials might be held to higher standards of concern for the general welfare, for example, than ordinary people. Or else those acting in official roles might be permitted or even required to do things which, considered from the point of view of individual morality, would be impermissible.

Both derivability and non-derivability are formally suited to explain either the addition or the removal of restrictions in public morality; both can therefore explain the appearance of discontinuity. The only way to decide between them is to see which form of explanation can be more plausibly filled out. I shall begin with a version of the derivability hypothesis, based on familiar concepts of individual morality. But while this can explain a good deal, it also leaves something out. I shall therefore go on to say what seems to me true in the non-derivability hypothesis, and this will involve giving an account of the alternative basis on which special conditions of public morality depend.

Even if public morality is not derivable from private, however, it does not mean that they are independent of one another. Both may derive from a common source that yields different results when applied to the generation of principles for action in the widely differing circumstances of private and public life. Neither private morality nor public morality is ultimate. Both result when the general constraints of morality are applied to certain types of action. Public morality would be derivable from private only if those constraints had to be applied first to the development of principles governing the conduct of persons acting individually, and could not be applied directly to public life. In that case one would have to reach the private principles from the general constraints of morality, and the public principles only from the private ones, as applied to public circumstances. But there is no a priori reason to think that ethics has this structure. If it does not, then public and private morality may share a common basis without one being derived from the other. I shall say more about this later. First I want to explore the more direct connections between them.

Part of my aim is to give a correct account of facts that are easily distorted by those defenders of political, diplomatic or military license who cloak themselves in the responsibilities of office.

Whoever denies the application of moral restraints to certain public decisions is making a moral claim, and a very strong one. But there is something to the idea of a moral discontinuity between private and public, and to understand the distortions we must know what this is.

III

Some of the moral peculiarity of official roles can be explained by the theory of obligation. Whoever takes on a public or official role assumes the obligation to serve a special function and often the interests of a special group. Like more personal obligations, this limits the claim that other sorts of reasons can make on him. Recall E. M. Forster's remark: 'I hate the idea of causes, and if I had to choose between betraying my country and betraying my friend, I hope I should have the courage to betray my country.'[2] He was not talking about public office, but similar problems can arise there. In a rigidly defined role like that of a soldier or judge or prison guard, only a very restricted set of considerations is supposed to bear on what one decides to do, and nearly all general considerations are excluded. With less definition, other public offices limit their occupants to certain considerations and free them from others, such as the good of mankind. Public figures sometimes even say and believe that they are obliged to consider only the national or state interest in arriving at their decisions as if it would be a breach of responsibility for them to consider anything else.

This apparent restriction on choice is easy to accept partly because, looked at from the other direction, it lifts restraints that might otherwise be burdensome. But any view as absolute as this is mistaken: there are no such extreme obligations, or offices to which they attach. One cannot, by joining the army, undertake an obligation to obey any order whatever from one's commanding officer. It is not possible to acquire an obligation to kill indebted gamblers by signing a contract as a Mafia hit man. It is not even possible to undertake a commitment to serve the interests of one's children in complete disregard of the interests of everyone else.

[2] 'What I Believe' in *Two Cheers for Democracy* (London, 1939).

Obligations to the state also have limits, which derive from their moral context.

Every obligation or commitment reserves some portion of the general pool of motivated action for a special purpose. Life being what it is, each person's supply of time, power, and energy is limited. The kinds of obligations one may undertake, and their limits, depend on how it is reasonable to allocate this pool, and how much liberty individuals should have to allocate it in radically uneven ways. This is true for personal obligations. It applies to public ones as well.

In private life some exclusivity is necessary if we are to allow people to form special relations and attachments, and to make special arrangements with each other on which they can rely. For similar reasons larger groups should be able to cooperate for mutual benefit, or to form social units that may have a geographical definition. And it is natural that the organization of such cooperative units will include institutions, roles, and offices and that the individuals in them will undertake obligations to serve the interests of the group in special ways – by promoting its prosperity, defending it against enemies, etc. To a degree, large-scale social arrangements can be seen as extensions of more individual obligations and commitments.

It may be that the added power conferred by an institutional role should be used primarily for the benefit of that institution and its constituents. The interests of mankind in general have a lesser claim on it. But this does not mean that prohibitions against harming others, directly or indirectly, are correspondingly relaxed. Just because the power to kill thousands of people is yours only because you are the secretary of defense of a certain country, it does not follow that you should be under no restrictions on the use of that power which do not derive specifically from your obligations to serve that country. The same reasoning that challenges private obligations that imply too much of a free hand in carrying them out, will also disallow public commitments with inadequate restraints on their greater power. Insofar as public obligations work like private ones, there is no reason to think that individuals in public roles are released from traditional moral requirements on the treatment of others, or that in public life, the end justifies the means.

IV

Let me now say what such an account leaves out. The moral impersonality of public action may be exaggerated and abused, but there is something in it, which a general theory of obligation cannot explain. Such a theory fails to explain why the *content* of public obligations differs systematically from that of private ones. The impersonality suitable for public action has two aspects: it implies both a heightened concern for results and a stricter requirement of impartiality. It warrants methods usually excluded for private individuals, and sometimes it licenses ruthlessness. This can be explained only by a direct application of moral theory to those public institutions[3] that create the roles to which public obligations are tied. To account for the difference between public and private life we must return to a point mentioned earlier: that public morality may be underivable from private not because they come from different sources, but because each of them contains elements derived independently from a common source.[4]

Morality is complicated at every level. My basic claim is that its impersonal aspects are more prominent in the assessment of institutions than in the assessment of individual actions, and that as a result, the design of institutions may include roles whose occupants must determine what to do by principles different from those that govern private individuals. This will be morally justified, however, by ultimate considerations that underlie individual morality as well. I shall present the view only in outline, and mostly without defending the moral opinions it expresses. My main contention is that the degree to which ruthlessness is acceptable in public life – the ways in which public actors may have to get their hands dirty – depends on moral features of the institutions through which public action is carried out.

Two types of concern determine the content of morality: con-

[3] What I say will be put in terms of the largest and most powerful institutions, the state and its agencies. But there is a wide range of public institutions including universities, political parties, charitable organizations, and revolutionary movements. Much of what I shall say about nation-states applies to these cases also in some degree. They too come under a kind of public morality.

[4] This retracts something I said at pp. 139–40 of 'Libertarianism without Foundations', 85 *Yale Law Journal* (1975).

cern with what will happen and concern with what one is doing.[5] Insofar as principles of conduct are determined by the first concern, they will be outcome-centered or consequentialist, requiring that we promote the best overall results. Insofar as they are determined by the second, the influence of consequences will be limited by certain restrictions on the means to be used, and also by a loosening of the requirement that one always pursue the best results. The action-centered aspects of morality include bars against treating others in certain ways which violate their rights, as well as the space allotted to each person for a life of his own, without the perpetual need to contribute to the general good in everything he does. Such provisions are described as action-centered because, while they apply to everyone, what they require of each person depends on his particular standpoint rather than on the impersonal consequentialist standpoint that surveys the best overall state of affairs and prescribes for each person whatever he can do to contribute to it.

The interaction and conflict between these two aspects of morality are familiar in private life. They result in a certain balance that emphasizes restrictions against harming or interfering with others, rather than requirements to benefit them, except in cases of serious distress. For the most part it leaves us free to pursue our lives and form particular attachments to some people, so long as we do not harm others.

When we apply the same dual conception to public institutions and activities, the results are different. There are several reasons for this. Institutions are not persons and do not have private lives, nor do institutional roles usually absorb completely the lives of their occupants. Public institutions are designed to serve purposes larger than those of particular individuals or families. They tend to pursue the interests of masses of people (a limiting case would be that of a world government, but most actual institutions have a less than universal constituency). In addition, public acts are diffused over many actors and sub-institutions; there is a division of labor both in execution and in decision. All this results in a different balance between the morality of outcomes and the morality of actions. These two types of moral constraint are differently

[5] I discuss this distinction in 'War and Massacre', *Philosophy & Public Affairs*, vol. I, No. 2 (1972) 123–44.

expressed in public life, and both of them take more impersonal forms.

Some of the same agent-centered restrictions on means will apply to public action as to private. But some of them will be weaker, permitting the public employment of coercive, manipulative, or obstructive methods that would not be allowable for individuals. There is some public analogue to the individual's right to lead his own life free of the constant demand to promote the best overall results, but it appears in the relations of states to one another rather than in their relations to their citizens: states can remain neutral in external disputes, and can legitimately favor their own populations – though not at any cost whatever to the rest of the world.

There is no comparable right of self-indulgence or favoritism for public officials or institutions vis-à-vis the individuals with whom they deal. Perhaps the most significant action-centered feature of public morality is a special requirement to treat people in the relevant population equally. Public policies and actions have to be much more impartial than private ones, since they usually employ a monopoly of certain kinds of power and since there is no reason in their case to leave room for the personal attachments and inclinations that shape individual lives.[6]

In respect to outcomes, public morality will differ from private in according them greater weight. This is a consequence of the weakening of certain action-centered constraints and permissions already described, which otherwise would have restrictive effects. The greater latitude about means in turn makes it legitimate to design institutions whose aim is to produce certain desirable results on a large scale, and to define roles in those institutions whose responsibility is mainly to further those results. Within the appropriate limits, public decisions will be justifiably more consequentialist than private ones. They will also have larger consequences to take into account.

To say that consequentialist reasons will be prominent is not to

---

[6] Would a giant with immense power be obliged to act primarily on impersonal grounds, if he were unique among millions of ordinary people whose lives he could affect? I doubt it. He would presumably have a personal life as well, which made some claims on him. The state is the closest thing we know to such a giant, and it is not similarly encumbered.

say what kinds of consequences matter. This is a well-worked field, and I shall avoid discussing the place of equality, liberty, autonomy and individual rights, as well as overall level of happiness, in a consequentialist view of the good. The point to remember is that consequentialist values need not be utilitarian; a consequentialist assessment of social institutions can be strongly egalitarian, in addition to valuing welfare, liberty, and individuality in themselves. Moreover, giving the members of a society the opportunity to lead their own lives free of consequentialist demands is one of the goods to be counted in a consequentialist social reckoning. But I won't try to present a complete system of public values here, for I am concerned with the more abstract claim that consequentialist considerations, together with impartiality, play a special role in the moral assessment and justification of public institutions.

The effect of these two deviations of public from private morality on the assessment of public action will be complex. The reason is that the constraints of public morality are not imposed as a whole in the same way on all public actions or on all public offices. Because public agency is itself complex and divided, there is a corresponding ethical division of labor, or ethical specialization. Different aspects of public morality are in the hands of different officials. This can create the illusion that public morality is more consequentialist or less restrictive than it is, because the general conditions may be wrongly identified with the boundaries of a particular role. But in fact those boundaries usually presuppose a larger institutional structure without which they would be illegitimate. (The most conspicuous example is the legitimacy conferred on legislative decisions by the limitation of constitutional protections enforced by the courts.)

By this rather complex route, the balance of outcome-oriented and action-oriented morality will justify the design of public institutions whose officials can do what would be unsuitable in private life. Some of the deviations will be conspicuously consequentialist: others will express the impersonality of public morality in other ways. Action-centered constraints will not be absent: there will still be restrictions on means. But those restrictions may be weaker in relation to the results than they are for individuals.

I have simply adapted a point made by Rawls in 'Two Concepts

of Rules'.[7] He argued that utilitarianism could justify practices
that exclude utilitarian reasoning in some circumstances. I am
arguing that a more complex morality than utilitarianism will
likewise have different implications for human conduct when
applied to its assessment directly and when applied indirectly via
the assessment of institutions through which action occurs. The
details of this morality cannot be explained here, but many of its
features depend on an idea of moral universality different from
that which underlies utilitarianism. Utilitarian assessment decides, basically, whether something is acceptable from a general
point of view that combines those of *all* individuals. The method
of combination is basically majoritarian. The alternative is to ask
whether something is acceptable from a schematic point of view
that represents in essentials the standpoint of each individual. The
method of combination here is a form of unanimity, since
acceptability from the schematic point of view represents acceptability to each person. Both of these moral conceptions can claim
to count everyone equally, yet they are very different. My own
opinion is that morality should be based on acceptability to each
rather than on acceptability to all. The problem is to define the two
points of view that express these opposed moral conceptions.[8]

It could also be said that the separate application of these basic
constraints to social institutions and to individual conduct yields
a moral division of labor between the individual and society, in
which individual and social ideals are inseparably linked. The
impersonal benevolence of public morality is intended to provide
a background against which individualism in private morality is
acceptable. It is a pressing and difficult question whether private
individualism and public benevolence are socially compatible, or
whether the tension between them makes this an unstable moral
conception and an unstable social ideal.

[7] *Philosophical Review* 64 (1955) 3–32.
[8] One attempt is made by Rawls in *A Theory of Justice* (Cambridge, Mass., 1971),
chap. III.

V

Because they are specialized, not all public institutions are equally sensitive to overall consequences. An important exception is the judiciary, at least in a society where the courts are designed to protect individual rights against both public and private encroachment. Neither the institution itself nor the roles it defines – judge, juror, prosecutor – are dominated by a concern with overall results. They act on narrower grounds. To some extent this narrowing of grounds is itself justified by consequentialist reasoning about the overall effects of such an institution. However the courts also embody the state's action-centered moral constraints – impersonal but not consequentialist. Very importantly, they are supposed to enforce its impartiality in serious dealings with individual citizens. And by setting limits to the means that can be employed by other public institutions, they leave those institutions free to concentrate more fully on achieving results within those limits.

To illustrate the positive claim that these limits differ from those that operate in private life, let me consider two familiar examples of public action: taxation and conscription. Both are imposed by the legislature in our society, and it may be thought that they are therefore indirectly consented to by the population. I believe it is a desperate measure to impute consent to everyone who is drafted or pays income taxes, on the ground that he votes or accepts certain public services. Consent is not needed to justify such legislative action, because the legislature is an institution whose authority to make such decisions on consequentialist grounds is morally justified in other ways. Its periodic answerability to the electorate is one feature of the institution (another being the constitutional protection of rights) that contributes to its legitimacy – but not by implying each citizen's consent to its actions.[9] Particularly when those actions are coercive the defense of consent is not credible.

Some would describe taxation as a form of theft and conscription as a form of slavery – in fact some would prefer to describe

[9] This conception of legitimacy is found in Thomas M. Scanlon, 'Nozick on Rights, Liberty, and Property', *Philosophy & Public Affairs*, vol. 6, No. 1 (1976) at pp. 17–20.

taxation as slavery too, or at least as forced labor.[10] Much might be said against these descriptions, but that is beside the point. For within proper limits, such practices when engaged in by governments are acceptable whatever they are called. If someone with an income of $2,000 a year trains a gun on someone with an income of $100,000 a year and makes him hand over his wallet, that is robbery. If the federal government withholds a portion of the second person's salary (enforcing the laws against tax evasion with threats of imprisonment under armed guard) and gives some of it to the first person in the form of welfare payments, food stamps, or free health care, that is taxation. In the first case it is (in my opinion) an impermissible use of coercive means to achieve a worthwhile end. In the second case the means are legitimate, because they are impersonally imposed by an institution designed to promote certain results. Such general methods of distribution are preferable to theft as a form of private initiative and also to individual charity. This is true not only for reasons of fairness and efficiency, but also because both theft and charity are disturbances of the relations (or lack of them) between individuals and involve their individual wills in a way that an automatic, officially imposed system of taxation does not. The results achieved by taxation in an egalitarian welfare state would not be produced either by a right of individual expropriation or by a duty of charity. Taxation therefore provides a case in which public morality is derived not from private morality, but from impersonal consequentialist considerations applied directly to public institutions, and secondarily to action within those institutions. There is no way of analyzing a system of redistributive taxation into the sum of a large number of individual acts all of which satisfy the requirements of private morality.

In the case of conscription, the coercion is extreme, and so is what one is forced to do. You are told to try to kill people who are trying to kill you, the alternative being imprisonment. Quite apart from fighting, military service involves unusual restrictions of liberty. Even assuming agreement about when conscription is acceptable and what exemptions should be allowed, this is a kind of coercion that it would be unthinkable to impose privately.

[10] E.g. Robert Nozick, *Anarchy, State, and Utopia* (New York, 1974) pp. 169–74.

A can't force B to help him fight a gang of hoodlums who are robbing them both, if B would rather give them his money. Again, the more impersonal viewpoint of public morality gives a different result.

But not everything is permitted. Restrictions on the treatment of individuals continue to operate from a public point of view, and they cannot be implemented entirely by the courts. One of the hardest lines to draw in public policy is the one that defines where the end stops justifying the means. If results were the only basis for public morality then it would be possible to justify anything, including torture and massacre, in the service of sufficiently large interests. Whether the limits are drawn by specific constitutional protections or not, the strongest constraints of individual morality will continue to limit what can be publicly justified even by extremely powerful consequentialist reasons.

VI

This completes my discussion of the continuities and discontinuities between public and private morality. I have argued that some of the special features of public morality can be explained in terms of a theory of obligation that also accounts for the steps individuals can take to restrict the grounds on which they will make certain choices. Public officials accept special obligations to serve interests that their offices are designed to advance – and to serve them in more or less well-defined ways. In doing so, they correlatively reduce their right to consider other factors, both their personal interests and more general ones not related to the institution or their role in it.

I have also argued, however, that the special character of public obligations – the weight they give both to results and to impartiality – reflects the relative impersonality of public action: its scale, its lack of individuality, its institutional structure. A theory of obligation explains only part of the change that occurs when an individual takes on a public role. It does not explain either the prominence of consequentialism or the shift in strength and character of action-centered reasons. I have tried to explain these differences as the result of a direct application of basic moral

constraints to public institutions and therefore to the public functions that individuals may undertake.

Both of these sources of public morality generate limits to what
a public official may do in the conduct of his office, even if he is
serving institutional interests. It is easy to forget about those
limits, for three reasons. First, restrictions against the use of public
power for private gain can seem like a moral cushion that insulates
whatever else is done officially from moral reproach. Second, the
fact that the holder of a public office takes on an obligation to a
particular group may foster the idea that he is obliged not to
consider anything except the interest of that group. Third, the
impersonal morality of public institutions, and the moral specialization that inevitably arises given the complexity of public
actions, lead naturally to the establishment of many roles whose
terms of reference are primarily consequentialist. Lack of attention
to the context that is necessary to make these roles legitimate can
lead to a rejection of all limits on the means thought to be justified
by ever greater ends. I have argued that these are all errors. It is
important to remember that they are *moral* views: the opinion that
in certain conditions a certain type of conduct is permissible has
to be criticized and defended by moral argument.

Let me return finally to the individuals who occupy public roles.
Even if public morality is not substantively derivable from private,
it applies to individuals. If one of them takes on a public role,
he accepts certain obligations, certain restrictions, and certain
limitations on what he may do. As with any obligation, this step
involves a risk that he will be required to act in ways incompatible
with other obligations or principles that he accepts. Sometimes
he will have to act anyway. But sometimes, if he can remember
them, he will see that the limits imposed by public morality itself
are being transgressed, and he is being asked to carry out a
judicial murder or a war of unjust aggression. At this point there
is no substitute for refusal and, if possible, resistance. Despite the
impersonal character of public morality and its complex application to institutions in which responsibility is divided, it tells us
not only how those institutions should be designed but also how
people in them should act. Someone who has committed public
wrongs in the exercise of his office can be just as guilty as a private
criminal. Sometimes his responsibility is partly absorbed by the

moral defects of the institution through which he acts; but the plausibility of that excuse is inversely proportional to the power and independence of the actor. Unfortunately this is not reflected in our treatment of former public servants who have often done far worse than take bribes.[11]

[11] I am grateful to Gerald Dworkin, Bernard Williams, and members of the Society for Ethical and Legal Philosophy for reactions to an earlier draft.

5 Rights, Goals, and Fairness*

T. M. SCANLON

Critics of utilitarianism frequently call attention to the abhorrent policies that unrestricted aggregative reasoning might justify under certain possible, or even actual, circumstances. They invite the conclusion that to do justice to the firm intuition that such horrors are clearly unjustifiable one must adopt a deontological moral framework that places limits on what appeals to maximum aggregate well-being can justify. As one who has often argued in this way, however, I am compelled to recognize that this position has its own weaknesses. In attacking utilitarianism one is inclined to appeal to individual rights, which mere considerations of social utility cannot justify us in overriding. But rights themselves need to be justified somehow, and how other than by appeal to the human interests their recognition promotes and protects? This seems to be the incontrovertible insight of the classical utilitarians. Further, unless rights are to be taken as defined by rather implausible rigid formulae, it seems that we must invoke what looks very much like the consideration of consequences in order to determine what they rule out and what they allow. Thus, for example, in order to determine whether a given policy violates the right of freedom of expression it is not enough to know merely that it restricts speech. We may need to consider also its effects: how it would affect access to the means of expression and what the consequences would be of granting to government the kind of regulatory powers it confers.

* The original version of this paper was presented at the Reisensberg Conference on Decision Theory and Social Ethics and appeared in an issue of *Erkenntnis* devoted to papers from that conference. This revised version is used with the permission of the editors of that journal and D. Reidel & Co. I am indebted to a number of people for critical comments and helpful discussion, particularly to Ronald Dworkin, Derek Parfit, Gilbert Harman, Samuel Scheffler, and Milton Wachsberg. Work on this paper was supported in part by a fellowship from the National Endowment for the Humanities.

I am thus drawn toward a two-tier view: one that gives an important role to consequences in the justification and interpretation of rights but which takes rights seriously as placing limits on consequentialist reasoning at the level of casuistry. Such a view looks like what has been called rule utilitarianism, a theory subject to a number of very serious objections. First, rule utilitarians are hard pressed to explain why, if at base they are convinced utilitarians, they are not thoroughgoing ones. How can they square their utilitarianism with the acceptance of individual actions that are not in accord with the utilitarian formula? Second, rule utilitarianism seems to be open to some of the same objections leveled against utilitarianism in its pure form; in particular it seems no more able than act utilitarianism is to give a satisfactory place to considerations of distributive justice. Third, in attempting to specify which rules it is that are to be applied in the appraisal of acts and policies, rule utilitarians of the usual sort are faced with an acute dilemma. If it is some set of ideal rules that are to be applied – those rules general conformity to which would have the best consequences – then the utilitarian case for a concern with rules, rather than merely with the consequences of isolated acts, appears lost. For this case must rest on benefits that flow from the general observance of rules but not from each individual act, and such benefits can be gained only if the rules are in fact generally observed. But if, on the other hand, the rules that are to be applied must be ones that are generally observed, the critical force of the theory seems to be greatly weakened.

The problem, then, is to explain how a theory can have, at least in part, a two-tier structure; how it can retain the basic appeal of utilitarianism, at least as it applies to the foundation of rights, and yet avoid the problems that have plagued traditional rule utilitarianism. As a start towards describing such a theory I will consider three questions. (1) What consequences are to be considered, and how is their value to be determined? (2) How do considerations of distributive justice enter the theory? (3) How does one justify taking rights (or various moral rules) as constraints on the production of valued consequences?

1. Consequences and their values

Here I have two remarks, one of foundation, the other of content. First, as I have argued elsewhere[1] but can here only assert, I depart from the classical utilitarians and many of their modern followers in rejecting subjective preferences as the basis for the valuation of outcomes. This role is to be played instead by an ethically significant, objective notion of the relative importance of various benefits and burdens.

Second, as to content, the benefits and burdens with which the theory is concerned must include not only the things that may happen to people but also factors affecting the ability of individuals to determine what will happen. Some of these factors are the concern of what are generally called rights, commonly[2] distinguished into (claim-) rights to command particular things, where others have a correlative duty to comply; liberties to do or refrain from certain things, where others have no such correlative duties; powers to change people's rights or status; and immunities from powers exercised by others. I take it to be the case that the familiar civil rights, as well as such things as rights of privacy and 'the right to life', are complexes of such elements. The de facto ability effectively to choose among certain options and the de facto absence of interference by others with one's choices are not the same thing as rights, although if it is generally believed that a person has a particular right, say a claim-right, this may contribute to his having such de facto ability or lack of interference. But, however they are created, such abilities and protections are important goods with which any moral theory must be concerned, and the allocation of rights is one way in which this importance receives theoretical recognition.

Any theory of right, since it deals with what agents should and may do, is in a broad sense concerned with the assignment of rights

---

[1] In 'Preference and Urgency', *The Journal of Philosophy* 72 (1975), pp. 655–70.

[2] Following Hohfeld and others. See W. N. Hohfeld, *Fundamental Legal Conceptions* (New Haven, 1923), and also Stig Kanger, 'New Foundations for Ethical Theory' in Risto Hilpinen, ed., *Deontic Logic: Introductory and Systematic Readings* (Dordrecht, 1971), pp. 36–58. On the distinction between concern with outcomes and concern with the allocation of competences to determine outcomes see Charles Fried, 'Two Concepts of Interests: Some Reflections of the Supreme Court's Balancing Test', *The Harvard Law Review* 76 (1963), p. 755–78.

and liberties. It is relevant to ask, concerning such a theory, how much latitude it gives a person in satisfying moral requirements and how much protection it gives a person through the constraints it places on the actions of others. Traditional utilitarianism has been seen as extreme on both these counts. It is maximally specific in the requirements it imposes on an agent, and, since there are no limits to what it may require to be done, it provides a minimum of reliable protection from interference by others. Objections to utilitarianism have often focused on its demanding and intrusive character,[3] and other theories of right may grant individuals both greater discretion and better protection. But these are goods with costs. When one individual is given a claim-right or liberty with respect to a certain option, the control that others are able to exercise over their own options is to some degree diminished. Further, if we take the assignment of rights to various individuals as, in at least some cases, an end-point of justification, then we must be prepared to accept the situation resulting from their exercise of these rights even if, considered in itself, it may be unattractive or at least not optimal. Both these points have been urged by Robert Nozick,[4] the latter especially in his attack on 'end-state' and 'patterned' theories. What follows from these observations, however, is not Nozick's particular theory of entitlements but rather a general moral about the kind of comparison and balancing that a justification of rights requires: the abilities and protections that rights confer must be assigned values that are comparable not only with competing values of the same kind but also with the values attached to the production of particular end-results.

The same moral is to be drawn from some of Bernard Williams' objections to utilitarianism.[5] Williams objects that utilitarianism, in demanding total devotion to the inclusive goal of maximum happiness, fails to give adequate recognition to the importance, for each individual, of the particular projects which give his life content. The problem with such an objection is that taken alone

---

[3] See Bernard Williams, 'A Critique of Utilitarianism', in J. J. C. Smart and B. Williams, *Utilitarianism: For and Against* (Cambridge, 1973).

[4] In *Anarchy, State and Utopia* (New York, 1974), esp. pp. 32–35 and Chapter 7.

[5] In Sec. 5 of 'A Critique of Utilitarianism'.

it may be made to sound like pure self-indulgence. Simply to demand freedom from moral requirements in the name of freedom to pursue one's individual projects is unconvincing. It neglects the fact that these requirements may protect interests of others that are at least as important as one's own. To rise clearly above the level of special pleading these objections must be made general. They must base themselves on a general claim about how important the interests they seek to protect are for any person as compared with the interests served by conflicting claims.

The two preceding remarks – of foundation and of content – are related in the following way. Since the ability to influence outcomes and protection from interference or control by others are things people care about, they will be taken into account in any subjective utilitarian theory. I will later raise doubts as to whether such a theory can take account of them in the right way, but my present concern is with the question what value is to be assigned to these concerns. On a subjective theory these values will be determined by the existing individual preferences in the society in question. I would maintain, however, that prevailing preferences are not an adequate basis for the justification of rights. It is not relevant, for example, to the determination of rights of religious freedom that the majority group in a society is feverishly committed to the goal of making its practices universal while the minority is quite tepid about all matters of religion. This is of course just an instance of the general objection to subjective theories stated above. The equally general response is that one has no basis on which to 'impose' values that run contrary to individual preferences. This objection draws its force from the idea that individual autonomy ought to be respected and that it is offensive to frustrate an individual's considered preferences in the name of serving his 'true interests'. This idea does not itself rest on preferences. Rather, it functions as the objective moral basis for giving preferences a fundamental role as the ground of ethically relevant valuations. But one may question whether this theoretical move is an adequate response to the intuitive idea from which it springs. To be concerned with individual autonomy is to be concerned with the rights, liberties and other conditions necessary for individuals to develop their own aims and interests and to make their preferences effective in shaping their own lives and

contributing to the formation of social policy. Among these will
be rights protecting people against various forms of paternalistic
intervention. A theory that respects autonomy will be one that
assigns all of these factors their proper weight. There is no reason
to think that this will be accomplished merely by allowing these
weights, and all others, to be determined by the existing
configuration of preferences.

2. Fairness and equality

Rather than speaking generally of 'distributive justice', which can
encompass a great variety of considerations, I will speak instead
of fairness, as a property of processes (e.g. of competitions), and
equality, as a property of resultant distributions. The question is
how these considerations enter a theory of the kind I am describing. One way in which a notion of equality can be built into
a consequentialist theory is through the requirement that, in
evaluating states of affairs to be promoted, we give equal consideration to the interests of every person. This principle of equal
consideration of interests has minimal egalitarian content. As
stated, it is compatible with classical utilitarianism which, after
all, 'counts each for one and none for more than one'. Yet many
have felt, with justification, that utilitarianism gives insufficient
weight to distributive considerations. How might this weight be
increased? Let me distinguish two ways. The first would be to
strengthen the principle of equal consideration of interests in such
a way as to make it incompatible with pure utilitarianism. 'Equal
consideration' could, for example, be held to mean that in any
justification by appeal to consequences we must give priority to
those individual interests that are 'most urgent'. To neglect such
interests in order to serve instead less urgent interests even of a
greater number of people would, on this interpretation, violate
'equality of consideration'. Adoption of this interpretation would
ward off some objections to utilitarianism based on its insensitivity
to distributive considerations but would at the same time preserve
other characteristic features of the doctrine, e.g. some of its
radically redistributive implications. Such a 'lexical interpretation'
has, of course, its own problems. Its strength (and plausibility)

is obviously dependent on the ranking we choose for determining the urgency of various interests.

The nature of such a ranking is an important problem, but one I cannot pursue here. Whatever the degree of distributive content that is built into the way individual interests are reckoned in moral argument, however, there is a second way in which distributive considerations enter a theory of the kind I wish to propose: equality of distributions and fairness of processes are among the properties that make states of affairs worth promoting. Equality in the distribution of particular classes of goods is at least sometimes of value as a means to the attainment of other valued ends, and in other cases fairness and equality are valuable in their own right.

Classical utilitarianism, of course, already counts equality as a means, namely as a means to maximum aggregate utility. Taken alone, this seems inadequate – too instrumental to account for the moral importance equality has for us. Yet I do think that in many of the cases in which we are most concerned with the promotion of equality we desire greater equality as a means to the attainment of some further end. In many cases, for example, the desire to eliminate great inequalities is motivated primarily by humanitarian concern for the plight of those who have least. Redistribution is desirable in large part because it is a means of alleviating their suffering (without giving rise to comparable suffering elsewhere). A second source of moral concern with redistribution in the contemporary world lies in the fact that great inequalities in wealth give to those who have more an unacceptable degree of control over the lives of others. Here again the case for greater equality is instrumental. Were these two grounds for redistribution to be eliminated (by, say, greatly increasing the standard of living of all concerned and preventing the gap between rich and poor, which remains unchanged, from allowing the rich to dominate) the moral case for equality would not be eliminated, but I believe that it would seem less pressing.

Beyond these and other instrumental arguments, fairness and equality often figure in moral argument as independently valuable states of affairs. So considered, they differ from the ends promoted in standard utilitarian theories in that their value does not rest on their being good things *for* particular individuals: fairness and equality do not represent ways in which individuals may be *better off*.[6] They are, rather, special morally desirable features of states of affairs or of social institutions. In admitting such moral features into the evaluation of consequences, the theory I am describing departs from standard consequentialist theories, which generally resist the introduction of explicitly moral considerations into the maximand. It diverges also from recent deontological theories, which bring in fairness and equality as specific moral requirements rather than as moral goals. I am inclined to pursue this 'third way' for several reasons.

First, it is not easy to come up with a moral argument for substantive equality (as distinct from mere formal equality or equal consideration of interests) which makes it look like an absolute moral requirement. Second, considerations of fairness and equality are multiple. There are many different processes that may be more or less fair, and we are concerned with equality in the distribution of many different and separable benefits and burdens. These are not all of equal importance; the strength of claims of equality and fairness depends on the goods whose distribution is at issue. Third, these claims do not seem to be absolute. Attempts to achieve equality or fairness in one area may conflict with the pursuit of these goals in other areas. In order to achieve greater equality we may, for example, change our processes in ways that involve unfairness in the handling of some individual cases. Perhaps the various forms of fairness and equality can be brought together under one all-encompassing notion of distributive justice which is always to be increased, but it is not obvious that this is so. In any event, it would remain the case that attempts to increase fairness and equality can have costs in other terms; they may interfere with processes whose efficiency is important to us, or involve unwelcome intrusions into individuals' lives. In such cases of conflict it does not seem that considerations of fairness and equality, as such, are always dominant. An increase in equality may in some cases not be worth its cost; whether it is will depend in part on what it is equality *of*.

---

[6] Here I am indebted to Kurt Baier. Defending the claim that fairness and equality are intrinsically valuable is of course a further difficult task. Perhaps all convincing appeals to these notions can be reduced to instrumental arguments, but I do not at present see how. Such a reduction would move my theory even closer to traditional utilitarianism.

Economists often speak of 'trade-offs' between equality and other concerns (usually efficiency). I have in the past been inclined, perhaps intolerantly, to regard this as crassness, but I am no longer certain that it is in principle mistaken. The suggestion that equality can be 'traded-off' against other goods arouses suspicion because it seems to pave the way for defenses of the status quo. Measures designed to decrease inequality in present societies are often opposed on the ground that they involve too great a sacrifice in efficiency or in individual liberty, and one way to head off such objections is to hold that equality is to be pursued whatever the cost. But one can hold that appeals to liberty and efficiency do not justify maintaining the status quo – and in fact that considerations of individual liberty provide some of the strongest arguments in favor of increased equality of income and wealth – without holding that considerations of equality are, as such, absolute and take priority over all other values.

3. Rights

Why give rights a special place in a basically consequentialist theory? How can a two-tier theory be justified? One common view of the place of rights, and moral rules generally, within utilitarianism holds that they are useful as means to the coordination of action. The need for such aids does not depend on imperfect motivation; it might exist even in a society of perfect altruists. A standard example is a rule regulating water consumption during a drought. A restriction to one bucket a day per household might be a useful norm for a society of utilitarians even though their reasons for taking more water than this would be entirely altruistic. Its usefulness does not depend on self-interest. But the value of such a rule does depend on the fact that the agents are assumed to act independently of one another in partial ignorance of what the others have done or will do. If Dudley knows what others will do, and knows that this will leave some water in the well, then there is no utilitarian reason why he should not violate the rule and take more than his share for some suitable purpose – as the story goes, to water the flowers in the public garden.

I am of two minds about such examples. On the one hand, I can feel the force of the utilitarian's insistence that if the water is not going to be used how can we object to Dudley's taking it? On the other hand, I do not find this line of reply wholly satisfying. Why should *he* be entitled to do what others were not? Well, because he knows and they didn't; he alone has the opportunity. But just because he has it does that mean he can exercise it unilaterally? Perhaps, to be unbearably priggish, he should call the surplus to the attention of the others so that they can all decide how to use it. If this alternative is available is it all right for him to pass it up and act on his own? A utilitarian might respond here that he is not saying that Dudley is entitled to do whatever he wishes with the surplus water; he is entitled to do with it what the principle of utility requires and nothing else.

Here a difference of view is shown. Permission to act outside the rule is seen by the non-utilitarian as a kind of freedom for the agent, an exemption, but it is seen by a utilitarian as a specific moral requirement. Dudley is required to do something that is different from what the others do because his situation is different, but he has no greater latitude for the exercise of discretion or personal preference than anyone else does. This suggests that one can look at an assignment of rights in either of two ways: as a way of constraining individual decisions in order to promote some desired further effect (as in the case of a system of rules defining a division of labor between co-workers) or as a way of parceling out valued forms of discretion over which individuals are in conflict. To be avoided, I think, is a narrow utilitarianism that construes all rights on the first model, e.g. as mechanisms of coordination or as hedges against individual errors in judgment. So construed, rights have no weight against deviant actions that can be shown to be the most effective way of advancing the shared goal.

If, however, the possibility of construing some rights on the second model is kept open, then rights can be given a more substantial role within a theory that is still broadly utilitarian. When, as seems plausible on one view of the water-shortage example, the purpose of an assignment of rights is to ensure an equitable distribution of a form of control over outcomes, then these rights are supported by considerations which persist even when contrary actions would promote optimum results. This could remain true for a society of conscientious (though perhaps not single-minded) consequentialists, provided that they are concerned with 'consequences' of the sort I have described above. But to say that a rule or a right is not in general subject to exceptions justified on act-utilitarian grounds is not to say that it is absolute. One can ask how important it is to preserve an equitable distribution of control of the kind in question, and there will undoubtedly be some things that outweigh this value. There is no point in observing the one-bucket restriction when the pump-house is on fire. Further, the intent of an assignment of rights on the second model is apt to be to forestall certain particularly tempting or likely patterns of behavior. If this is so, there may be some acts which are literally contrary to the formula in which the right is usually stated but which do not strike us as actual violations of the right. We are inclined to allow them even though the purposes they serve may be less important than the values the right is intended to secure. Restrictions on speech which nonetheless are not violations of freedom of expression are a good example of such 'apparent exceptions'.

Reflections of this kind suggest to me that the view that there is a moral right of a certain sort is generally backed by something like the following:

(i) An empirical claim about how individuals would behave or how institutions would work in the absence of this particular assignment of rights (claim-rights, liberties, etc.).

(ii) A claim that this result would be unacceptable. This claim will be based on valuation of consequences of the sort described in section 1 above, taking into account also considerations of fairness and equality.

(iii) A further empirical claim about how the envisaged assignment of rights will produce a different outcome.

The empirical parts of this schema play a larger or at least more conspicuous role in some rights than in others. In the case of the right to freedom of expression this role is a large one and fairly well recognized. Neglecting this empirical element leads rights to degenerate into implausible rigid formulae. The impossibility of taking such a formula literally, as defining an absolute moral bar, lends plausibility to a 'balancing' view, according to which such a right merely represents one important value among others, and decisions must be reached by striking the proper balance between them. Keeping in mind the empirical basis of a right counters this tendency and provides a ground (1) for seeing that 'apparent exceptions' of the kind mentioned above are not justified simply by balancing one right against another; (2) for seeing where genuine balancing of interests is called for and what its proper terms are; and (3) for seeing how the content of a right must change as conditions change. These remarks hold, I think, not only for freedom of expression but also for other rights, for example, rights of due process and rights of privacy. In each of these cases a fairly complex set of institutional arrangements and assumptions about how these arrangements operate stands, so to speak, between the formula through which the right is identified and the goals to which it is addressed. This dependence on empirical considerations is less evident in the case of rights, like the right to life, that lie more in the domain of individual morality. I will argue below, however, that this right too can profitably be seen as a system of authorizations and limitations of discretion justified on the basis of an argument of the form just described.

This view of rights is in a broad sense consequentialist in that it holds rights to be justified by appeal to the states of affairs they promote. It seems to differ from the usual forms of rule utilitarianism, however, in that it does not appear to be a maximizing doctrine. The case for most familiar rights – freedom of expression, due process, religious toleration – seems to be more concerned with the avoidance of particular bad consequences than with promoting maximum benefit. But this difference is in part only apparent. The dangers that these rights are supposed to ward off are major ones, not likely to be overshadowed by everyday considerations. Where they are overshadowed, the theory I have described allows for the rights in question to be set aside. Further, the justification for the particular form that such a right takes allows for the consideration of costs. If a revised form of some right would do the intended job as well as the standard form at clearly reduced costs to peripheral interests, then this form would obviously be preferred. It should be noted, however, that if something is being maximized here it can not, in view of the role that the goals of fairness and equality play in the theory, be simply the sum of individual benefits. Moreover, this recognition of an element of maximization does not mean that just any possible improvement in the way people generally behave will become the subject of a right. Rights concern the alleviation of certain major problems, and incremental gains in other goods become relevant to rights in the way just mentioned only when they flow from improvements in our ways of dealing with such problems.

I have suggested that the case for rights derives in large part from the goal of promoting an acceptable distribution of control over important factors in our lives. This general goal is one that would be of importance to people in a wide range of societies. But the particular rights it calls for may vary from society to society. Thus, in particular, the rights we have on the view I have proposed are probably not identical with the rights that would be recognized under the system of rules, general conformity to which in our society would have the best consequences. The problems to which our rights are addressed are ones that arise given the distribution of power and the prevailing patterns of motivation in the societies in which we live. These problems may not be ones that would arise were an ideal code of behaviour to prevail.[7] (And they might not be the same either as those we would face in a 'state of nature'.) Concern with rights does not involve accepting these background conditions as desirable or as morally unimpeachable; it only involves seeing them as relatively fixed features of the environment with which we must deal.

[7] How much this separates my view of rights from an ideal rule utilitarian theory will depend on how that theory construes the notion of an ideal system of rules being 'in force' in a society. In Brandt's sophisticated version, for example, what is required is that it be true, and known in the society, that a high proportion of adults subscribe to these rules, that is, chiefly, that they are to some extent motivated to avoid violating the rules and feel guilty when they believe they have done so. ('Some Merits of One Form of Rule Utilitarianism' in Gorovitz, ed., *Mill: Utilitarianism, with Critical Essays* [Indianapolis, Ind., 1971].) This may not insure that the level of conformity with these rules is much greater than the level of moral behavior in societies we are familiar with. If it does not, then Brandt's theory may not be much more 'ideal' than the theory of rights offered here. The two theories appear to differ, however, on the issues discussed in sections 1 and 2 above. These issues also divide my view from R. M. Hare's version of rule utilitarianism, with which I am otherwise in much agreement. See his 'Ethical Theory and Utilitarianism', in H. D. Lewis, ed., *Contemporary British Philosophy, Fourth Series* (London, 1976). Like these more general theories, the account of rights offered here has a great deal in common with the view put forward by Mill in the final chapter of *Utilitarianism* (particularly if Mill's remarks about 'justice' are set aside).

Which features of one's society are to be held fixed in this way for purposes of moral argument about rights? This can be a controversial moral question and presents a difficult theoretical issue for anyone holding a view like rule utilitarianism. As more and more is held fixed, including more about what other agents are in fact doing, the view converges toward act utilitarianism. If, on the other hand, very little is held fixed then the problems of ideal forms of rule utilitarianism seem to loom larger: we seem to risk demanding individual observance of rights when this is pointless given the lack of general conformity.

This dilemma is most acute to the degree that the case for rights (or moral rules) is seen to rest on their role in promoting maximum utility through the coordination of individual action. Where this is actually the case – as it is with many rules and perhaps some rights – it is of undoubted importance what others are in fact doing – to what degree these rights and rules are generally observed and how individual action will affect general observance. I suggest, however, that this is not the case with most rights. On the view I propose, a central concern of most rights is the promotion and maintenance of an acceptable distribution of control over important factors in our lives. Where a certain curtailment of individual discretion or official authority is clearly required for this purpose, the fact that this right is not generally observed does not undermine the case for its observance in a given instance. The case against allowing some to dictate the private religious observances of others, for example, does not depend on the existence of a general practice of religious toleration. Some of the benefits at which rights of religious freedom are aimed – the benefits of a general climate of religious toleration – are secured only when there is general compliance with these rights. But the case for enforcing these rights does not depend in every instance on these benefits.

For these reasons, the view of rights I have proposed is not prey to objections often raised against ideal rule utilitarian theories. A further question is whether it is genuinely distinct from an act-consequentialist doctrine. It may seem that, for reasons given above, it cannot be: if an act in violation of a given right yields some consequence that is of greater value than those with which the right is concerned, then on my view the right is to be set aside.

If the act does not have such consequences then, in virtue of its conflict with the right and the values that right protects, it seems that the act would not be justifiable on act-consequentialist grounds anyway. But this rests on a mistake. The values supporting a particular right need not all stand to be lost in every case in which the right is violated. In defending the claim that there is a right of a certain sort, e.g., a particular right of privacy, we must be prepared to compare the advantages of having this right – the advantages, e.g., of being free to decline to be searched – against competing considerations – e.g., the security benefits derived from a more lenient policy of search and seizure. But what stands to be gained or lost in any given instance in which a policeman would like to search me need not coincide with either of these values. It may be that in that particular case I don't care.[8]

There is, then, no incoherence in distinguishing between the value of having a right and the cost of having it violated on a particular occasion. And it is just the values of the former sort that we must appeal to in justifying a two-tier view. What more can be said about these values? From an act-consequentialist point of view the value attached to the kind of control and protection that rights confer seems to rest on mistrust of others. If everyone could be relied upon to do the correct thing from an act-consequentialist standpoint would we still be so concerned with rights? This way of putting the matter obscures several important elements. First, it supposes that we can all agree on the best thing to be done in each case. But concern with rights is based largely on the warranted supposition that we have significantly differing ideas of the good and that we are interested in the freedom to put our own conceptions into practice. Second, the objection assumes that we are concerned only with the correct choice being made and have no independent concern with who makes it. This also seems clearly false. The independent value we attach to being able to make our own choices should, however, be distinguished from the further value we may attach to having it recognized that we are *entitled* to make them. This we may also value in itself as a sign of respect and personhood, but there is a question to what degree this value is an artifact of our moral beliefs and customs rather than a basis

---

[8] On the importance of establishing the proper terms of balancing see Fried, 'Two Concepts of Interests', p. 758.

for them. Where a moral framework of rights is established and recognized, it will be important for a person to have his status as a right holder generally acknowledged. But is there something analogous to this importance that is lost for everyone in a society of conscientious act consequentialists where no one holds rights? It is not clear to me that there is, but, however this may be, my account emphasizes the value attached to rights for the sake of what they may bring rather than their value as signs of respect.

If the factors just enumerated were the whole basis for concern with rights then one would expect the case for them to weaken and the force of act-consequentialist considerations to grow relatively stronger as (1) the importance attached to outcomes becomes absolutely greater and hence, presumably, also relatively greater as compared with the independent value of making choices one's self, and as (2) the assignment of values to the relevant outcomes becomes less controversial. To some extent both these things happen in cases where life and death are at stake, and here mistrust emerges as the more plausible basis for concern with rights.

4. Cases of life and death

From the point of view suggested in this paper, the right to life is to be seen as a complex of elements including particular liberties to act in one's own defense and to preserve one's life, claim-rights to aid and perhaps to the necessities of life, and restrictions on the liberty of others to kill or endanger. Let me focus here on elements in these last two categories, namely limits on the liberty to act in ways that lead to a person's death. An act-consequentialist standard could allow a person to take action leading to the death of another whenever this is necessary to avoid greater loss of life elsewhere. Many find this policy too permissive, and one explanation of this reaction is that it represents a kind of blind conservatism. We know that our lives are always in jeopardy in many ways. Tomorrow I may die of a heart attack or a blood clot. I may be hit by a falling tree or discover that I have a failing liver or find myself stood up against a wall by a group of terrorists. But we are reluctant to open the door to a further form of deadly risk by licensing others to take our life should this be necessary to minimize loss of life overall. We are reluctant to do this even when the effect would be to increase our net chances of living a long life by decreasing the likelihood that we will actually die when one of the natural hazards of life befalls us. We adopt, as it were, the attitude of hoping against hope not to run afoul of any of these hazards, and we place less stock on the prospect of escaping alive should we be so unlucky. It would not be irrational for a person to *decide* to increase his chances of survival by joining a transplant-insurance scheme, i.e. an arrangement guaranteeing one a heart or kidney should he need one provided he agrees to sacrifice himself to become a donor if he is chosen to do so. But such a decision is sufficiently controversial and the stakes so high that it is not a decision that can be taken to have been made for us as part of a unanimously acceptable basis for the assignment of rights. What I have here called conservatism is, however, uncomfortably close to a bias of the lucky against the unlucky insofar as it rests on a conscious turning of attention away from the prospect of our being one of the unlucky ones.

A substitute for conservatism is mistrust. We are reluctant to place our life in *anyone's* hands. We are even more reluctant to place our lives in *everyone's* hands as the act-consequentialist standard would have us do. Such mistrust is the main factor supporting the observed difference between the rationality of joining a voluntary transplant-insurance scheme and the permissibility of having a compulsory one (let alone the universally administered one that unrestricted act consequentialism could amount to). A person who joins a voluntary scheme has the chance to see who will be making the decisions and to examine the safeguards on the process. In assessing the force of these considerations one should also bear in mind that what they are to be weighed against is not 'the value of life itself' but only a small increase in the probability of living a somewhat longer life.

These appeals to 'conservatism' and mistrust, if accepted, would support something like the distinction between killing and letting die: we are willing to grant to others the liberty not to save us from threat of death when this is necessary to save others, but we are unwilling to license them to put us under threat of death when we have otherwise escaped it. As is well known, however, the killing/letting die distinction appears to permit some actions leading to a person's death that are not intuitively permissible. These are actions in which an agent refrains from aiding someone already under threat of death and does so because that person's death has results he considers advantageous. (I will assume that they are thought advantageous to someone other than the person who is about to die.) The intuition that such actions are not permitted would be served by a restriction on the liberty to fail to save, specifying that this course of action cannot be undertaken on the basis of conceived advantages of having the person out of the way. Opponents of the law of double effect have sometimes objected that it is strange to make the permissibility of an action depend on quite subtle features of its rationale. In the context of the present theory, however, the distinction just proposed is not formally anomalous. Conferrals of authority and limitations on it often take the form not simply of licensing certain actions or barring them but rather of restricting the grounds on which actions can be undertaken. Freedom of expression embodies restrictions of this kind, for example, and this is one factor responsible for the distinction between real and apparent violations mentioned above.[9]

Reasons for such a restriction in the present case are easy to come by. People have such powerful and tempting reasons for wanting others removed from the scene that it is obviously a serious step to open the door to calculations taking these reasons into account. Obviously, what would be proposed would be a qualified restriction, allowing consideration of the utilitarian, but not the purely self-interested, advantages to be gained from a person's death. But a potential agent's perception of this distinction does not seem to be a factor worth depending on.

The restriction proposed here may appear odd when compared to our apparent policy regarding mutual aid. If, as seems to be the case, we are prepared to allow a person to fail to save another when doing so would involve a moderately heavy sacrifice, why not allow him to do the same for the sake of a much greater benefit, to be gained from that person's death? The answer seems to be that, while a principle of mutual aid giving less consideration to

[9] For a view of freedom of expression embodying this feature, see Scanlon, 'A Theory of Freedom of Expression', *Philosophy and Public Affairs* I (1972), p. 204–26.

the donor's sacrifice strikes us as too demanding, it is not nearly as threatening as a policy allowing one to consider the benefits to be gained from a person's death.

These appeals to 'conservatism' and mistrust do not seem to me to provide adequate justification for the distinctions in question. They may explain, however, why these distinctions have some appeal for us and yet remain matters of considerable controversy.

6 Liberalism

RONALD DWORKIN

I

In this essay I shall propose a theory about what liberalism is; but I face an immediate problem. My project supposes that there is such a thing as liberalism, and the opinion is suddenly popular that there is not. Relatively recently – sometime before the Vietnam War – politicians who called themselves 'liberals' held certain positions that could be identified as a group. Liberals were for greater economic equality, for internationalism, for freedom of speech and against censorship, for greater equality between the races and against segregation, for a sharp separation of church and state, for greater procedural protection for accused criminals, for decriminalization of 'morals' offenses, particularly drug offenses and consensual sexual offenses involving only adults, and for an aggressive use of central government power to achieve all these goals. These were, in the familiar phrase, liberal 'causes', and those who promoted these causes could be distinguished from another large party of political opinion that could usefully be called 'conservative'. Conservatives tended to hold the contrary position to each of the classical liberal causes.

But a series of developments have called into question whether liberalism is in fact a distinct political theory. One of these was the war. Kennedy and his men called themselves liberals; so did Johnson, who retained the Kennedy men and added liberals of his own. But the war was inhumane, and discredited the idea that liberalism was the party of humanity. It would have been possible to argue, of course, that the Bundys and McNamaras and Rostows were false liberals, who sacrificed liberal principles for the sake of personal power, or incompetent liberals who did not understand that liberal principles prohibited what they did. But many critics drew the different conclusion that the war had exposed hidden connections between liberalism and exploitation. Once these supposed connections were exposed, they were seen to include domestic as well as external exploitation, and the line between liberalism and conservatism was then thought to be sham.

Second, politics began to produce issues that seemed no longer to divide into liberal and conservative positions. It is not clear, for example, whether concern for protecting the environment from pollution, even at the cost of economic growth that might reduce unemployment, is a liberal cause or not. Consumer protection appeals equally to consumers who call themselves liberal and those who say they are conservative. Many different groups – not only environmentalists and consumer protectionists – now oppose what is called the growth mentality, that is, the assumption that it should be an important aim of government to improve the total wealth or product of the country. It is also fashionable to ask for more local control by small groups over political decisions, not so much because decisions made locally are likely to be better, but because personal political relationships of mutual respect and cooperation, generated by local decisions, are desirable for their own sake. Opposition to growth for its own sake, and opposition to the concentration of power, seem liberal in spirit because liberals traditionally opposed the growth of big business and traditionally supported political equality. But these positions nevertheless condemn the strategies of central economic and political organization that have, certainly since the New Deal, been thought to be distinctly liberal strategies.

Third, and in consequence, politicians are less likely than before to identify themselves as 'liberal' or 'conservative', and more likely to combine political positions formerly thought liberal with those formerly thought conservative. President Carter, for example, professes what seem to be 'liberal' positions on human rights with 'conservative' positions on the importance of balancing the national budget even at the expense of improved welfare programs, and many commentators attribute his unanticipated nomination to his ability to break through political categories in this way. In Britain as well new combinations of old positions have appeared: the present Labour government seems no more 'liberal' than the Tories on matters of censorship, for example, and

scarcely more liberal on matters of immigration or police procedures. Citizens, too, seem to have switched positions while
retaining labels. Many who now call themselves 'liberal' support
causes that used to be conservative: it is now self-identified
'liberals' who want to curtail the regulatory power of the national
executive. Politicians and analysts, it is true, continue to use the
old categories: they debate, for example, whether Carter is 'really'
a liberal, and some of them (like George McGovern at a recent
meeting of Americans for Democratic Action) still propose to
speak for American 'liberals'. But the categories seem to many
much more artificial than they did.

I want to argue that a certain conception of equality, which I
shall call the liberal conception of equality, is the nerve of liberalism. But that supposes that liberalism is an authentic and
coherent political morality, so that it can make sense to speak of
'its' central principle, and these developments may be taken to
suggest that that is not. They may seem to support the following
sceptical thesis instead. 'The word "liberalism" has been used,
since the eighteenth century, to describe various distinct clusters
of political positions, but with no important similarity of principle among the different clusters called "liberal" at different
times. The explanation of why different clusters formed in various
circumstances, or why they were called "liberal", cannot be found
by searching for any such principle. It must be found instead in
complicated accidents of history, in which the self-interest of
certain groups, the prevalence of certain political rhetoric, and
many other discrete factors played different parts. One such
cluster was formed, for such reasons, in the period of the New
Deal: it combined an emphasis on less inequality and greater
economic stability with more abundant political and civil liberty
for the groups then campaigning for these goals. Our contemporary notion of "liberal" is formed from that particular package
of political aims.

'But the forces that formed and held together that package have
now been altered in various ways. Businessmen, for example, have
now come to see that various elements in the package – particularly those promoting economic stability – work very much
in their favor. White working men have come to see that certain
sorts of economic and social equality for racial minorities threaten

their own interests. Political liberties have been used, not merely or even mainly by those anxious to achieve the limited economic equality of the New Deal, but also by social rebels who threaten ideals of social order and public decency that the old liberal did not question. The question of Israel, and Soviet violations of the rights of intellectuals, have led the old liberal to withdraw his former tolerance for the Soviet Union and the expansion of its power. So New Deal "liberalism", as a package of political positions, is no longer an important political force. Perhaps a new cluster of positions will form which will be called "liberal" by its supporters and critics. Perhaps not. It does not much matter, because the new cluster, whether it is called liberalism or not, will bear no important connections of principle to the old liberalism. The idea of liberalism, as a fundamental political theory that produced the package of liberal causes, is a myth with no explanatory power whatsoever.'

That is the sceptic's account. There is, however, an alternative account of the break up of the liberal package of ideas. In any coherent political program there are two elements: constitutive political positions that are valued for their own sake, and derivative positions that are valued as strategies, as means of achieving the constitutive positions.[1] The sceptic believes that the liberal

---

[1] I shall provide, in this footnote, a more detailed description of this distinction. A comprehensive political theory is a structure in which the elements are related more or less systematically, so that very concrete political positions (like the position that income taxes should now be raised or reduced) are the consequences of more abstract positions (like the position that large degrees of economic inequality should be eliminated) that are in turn the consequences of still more abstract positions (like the position that a community should be politically stable) that may be the consequences of more abstract positions still. It would be unrealistic to suppose that ordinary citizens and politicians, or even political commentators or theoreticians, organize their political convictions in that way; yet anyone who supposes himself to take political decisions out of principle would recognize that some such organization of his full position must be possible in principle.

We may therefore distinguish, for any full political theory, between constitutive and derivative political positions. A constitutive position is a political position valued for its own sake: a political position such that any failure fully to secure that position, or any decline in the degree to which it is secured, is *pro tanto* a loss in the value of the overall political arrangement. A derivative political position is a position that is not, within the theory in question, constitutive.

A constitutive position is not necessarily absolute, within any theory, because a theory may contain different and to some degree antagonistic constitutive positions. Even though a theory holds, for example, that a loss in political equality

package of ideas had no constitutive political morality at all; it was a package formed by accident and held together by self-interest. The alternate account argues that the package had a constitutive morality, and has come apart, to the extent it has, because it has become less clear which derivative positions best serve that constitutive morality.

On this account, the break up of New Deal liberalism was the consequence, not of any sudden disenchantment with that fundamental political morality, but rather of changes in opinion and circumstance that made it doubtful whether the old strategies for enforcing that morality were right. If this alternate account

is *pro tanto* a loss in the justice of a political arrangement, it may nevertheless justify that loss in order to improve prosperity, because overall economic prosperity is also a constitutive position within the theory. In that case, the theory might recommend a particular economic arrangement (say a mixed capitalistic and socialistic economy) as the best compromise between two constitutive political positions, neither of which may properly be ignored. Neither equality nor overall well-being would be absolute, but both would be constitutive, because the theory would insist that if some means *could* be found to reach the same level of prosperity without limiting equality, then that result would be an improvement in justice over the compromise that is, unfortunately, necessary. If, on the other hand, the theory recognized that free enterprise was on the whole the best means of securing economic prosperity, but stood ready to abandon free enterprise, with no sense of any compromise, on those few occasions when free enterprise is not efficient, then free enterprise would be, within that theory, a derivative position. The theory would not argue that if some other means of reaching the same prosperity could be found, without curtailing free enterprise, that other means would be superior; if free enterprise is only a derivative position, then the theory is indifferent whether free enterprise or some other derivative position is sacrificed to improve the overall state-of-affairs. We must be careful to distinguish the question of whether a particular position is constitutive within a theory from the different question of whether the theory insulates the position by arguing that it is wrong to reexamine the value of the position on particular occasions. A theory may provide that some derivative positions should be more or less insulated from sacrifice on specified occasions, even when officials think that such a sacrifice would better serve constitutive positions, in order better to protect these constitutive goals in the long run. Rule utilitarianism is a familiar example, but the constitutive goals to be protected need not be utilitarian. A fundamentally egalitarian political theory might take political equality (one man, one vote) as an insulated though derivative position, not allowing officials to rearrange voting power to reach what they take to be a more fundamental equality in the community, because a more fundamental equality will be jeopardized rather than served by allowing tinkering with the franchise. Insulated derivative positions need not be absolute – a theory may provide that even an insulated position may be sacrificed, with no loss in overall justice even *pro tanto*, when the gain to constitutive positions is sufficiently apparent and pronounced. But insulated positions might be made absolute without losing their character as derivative.

is correct, then the ideal of liberalism as a fundamental political morality is not only not a myth, but is an idea necessary to any adequate account of modern political history, and to any adequate analysis of contemporary political debate. That conclusion will, of course, appeal to those who continue to think of themselves as liberals. But it must also be the thesis of critics of liberalism; at least of those who suppose that liberalism, in its very nature, is exploitative, or destructive of important values of community, or in some other way malign. For these comprehensive critics, no less than partisans, must deny that the New Deal liberal settlement was a merely accidental coincidence of political positions.

But of course we cannot decide whether the sceptical account or this alternative account is superior until we provide, for the latter, some theory about which elements of the liberal package are to be taken as constitutive and which derivative. Unfortunately liberals and their critics disagree, both between and within the two groups, about that very issue. Critics often say, for example, that liberals are committed to economic growth, to the bureaucratic apparatus of government and industry necessary for economic growth, and to the form of life in which growth is pursued for its own sake, a form of life that emphasises competition, individualism and material satisfactions. It is certainly true that politicians whom we consider paradigmatic liberals, like Hubert Humphrey and Roy Jenkins, emphasized the need for economic growth. But is this emphasis on growth a matter of constitutive principle because liberalism is tied to some form of utilitarianism that makes overall prosperity a good in itself? If so, then the disenchantment of many liberals with the idea of growth argues from the sceptical view that liberalism was a temporary alliance of unrelated political positions that has now been abandoned. Or is it a matter of derivative strategy within liberal theory – a debatable strategy for reducing economic inequality, for example – and therefore a matter on which liberals might disagree without deep schism or crisis? This question cannot be answered simply by pointing to the conceded fact that many who call themselves liberals once supported economic development more enthusiastically than they do now, any more than it can be shown that there is a connection of principle between imperialism and liberalism simply by naming men who called themselves liberals and were among those responsible for Vietnam. The vital questions here are questions of theoretical connection, and simply pointing at history, without at least some hypothesis about the nature of those connections, is useless.

The same question must be raised about the more general issue of the connection between liberalism and capitalism. It is certainly true that most of those who have called themselves liberals, both in America and Britain, have been anxious to make the market economy more fair in its workings and results, or to mix a market and collective economy, rather than to replace the market economy altogether with a plainly socialist system. That is the basis for the familiar charge that there is no genuine difference, within the context of western politics, between liberals and conservatives. But once again different views about the connection between capitalism and liberalism are possible. It may be that the constitutive positions of New Deal liberalism must include the principle of free enterprise itself, or principles about liberty that can only be satisfied by a market economy for conceptual reasons. If so, then any constraints on the market the liberal might accept, through redistribution or regulation or a mixed economy, would be a compromise with basic liberal principles, perhaps embraced out of practical necessity in order to protect the basic structure from revolution. The charge, that the ideological differences between liberalism and conservatism are relatively unimportant, would be supported by that discovery. If someone was persuaded to abandon capitalism altogether, he would no longer be a liberal; if many former liberals did so, then liberalism would be crippled as a political force. But perhaps, on the contrary, capitalism is not constitutive but derivative in New Deal liberalism. It might have been popular among liberals because it seemed (rightly or wrongly) the best means of achieving different and more fundamental liberal goals. In that case, liberals can disagree about whether free enterprise is worth preserving under new circumstances, again without theoretical crisis or schism, and the important ideological difference from conservatives may still be preserved. Once again, we must give attention to the theoretical question in order to frame hypotheses with which to confront the political facts.

These two issues – the connection of liberalism with economic growth and capitalism – are especially controversial, but we can locate similar problems of distinguishing what is fundamental from what is strategic in almost every corner of the New Deal liberal settlement. The liberal favors free speech. But is free speech a fundamental value, or is it only a means to some other goal like the discovery of truth (as Mill argued) or the efficient functioning of democracy (as Michaeljohn suggested)? The liberal disapproves of enforcing morality through the criminal law. Does this suggest that liberalism opposes the formation of a shared community sense of decency? Or is liberalism hostile only to using the criminal law to secure that shared community sense? I must say, perhaps out of unnecessary caution, that these questions cannot be answered, at the end of the day, apart from history and developed social theory; but it does not contradict that truism to insist that philosophical analysis of the idea of liberalism is an essential part of that very process.

So my original question – what is liberalism – turns out to be a question that must be answered, at least tentatively, before the more clearly historical questions posed by the sceptical thesis can be confronted. For my question is just the question of what morality is constitutive in particular liberal settlements like the New Deal package.

My project does take a certain view of the role of political theory in politics. It supposes that liberalism consists in some constitutive political morality that has remained roughly the same over some time, and that continues to be influential in politics. It supposes that distinct liberal settlements are formed when, for one reason or another, those moved by that constitutive morality settle on a particular scheme of derivative positions as appropriate to complete a practical liberal political theory, and others, for their own reasons, become allies in promoting that scheme. Such settlements break up, and liberalism is accordingly fragmented, when these derivative positions are discovered to be ineffective, or when economic or social circumstances change so as to make them ineffective, or when the allies necessary to make an effective political force are no longer drawn to the scheme. I do not mean that the constitutive morality of liberalism is the only force at work in forming liberal settlements, or even that it is the most powerful, but only that it is sufficiently distinct and influential to give sense to the idea, shared by liberals and their critics, that liberalism exists, and to give sense to the popular practice of arguing about what it is.

But the argument so far has shown that the claim that a particular position is constitutive rather than derivative in a political theory will be both controversial and complex. How shall I proceed? Any satisfactory description of the constitutive morality of liberalism must meet the following catalogue of conditions. (a) It must state positions that it makes sense to suppose might be constitutive of political programs for people in our culture. I do not claim simply that some set of constitutive principles could explain liberal settlements if people held those principles, but that a particular set does help to explain liberal settlements because people actually have held those principles. (b) It must be sufficiently well tied to the last clear liberal settlement – the political positions I described at the outset as acknowledged liberal 'causes' – so that it can be seen to be constitutive for that entire scheme; so that the remaining positions in the scheme can be seen, that is, to be derivative given that constitutive morality. (c) It must state constitutive principles in sufficient detail so as to discriminate a liberal political morality from other, competing political moralities. If, for example, I say simply that it is constitutive of liberalism that the government must treat its citizens with respect, I have not stated a constitutive principle in sufficient detail, because, although liberals might argue that all their political schemes follow from that principle, conservatives, Marxists and perhaps even fascists would make the same claim for their theories. (d) Once these requirements of authenticity, completeness and distinction are satisfied, then a more comprehensive and frugal statement of constitutive principles meeting these requirements is to be preferred to a less comprehensive and frugal scheme, because the former will have greater explanatory power, and provide a fairer test of the thesis that these constitutive principles both precede and survive particular settlements.

The second of these four conditions provides a starting point. I must therefore repeat the list of what I take to be the political positions of the last liberal settlement, and I shall, for convenience, speak of 'liberals' as these who support those positions. In economic policy, liberals demand that inequalities of wealth be reduced through welfare and other forms of redistribution financed by progressive taxes. They believe that government should intervene in the economy to promote economic stability, to control inflation, to reduce unemployment, and to provide services that would not otherwise be provided, but they favor a pragmatic and selective intervention over a dramatic change from free enterprise to wholly collective decisions about investment, production, prices and wages. They support racial equality, and approve government intervention to secure it, through constraints on both public and private discrimination in education, housing and employment. But they oppose other forms of collective regulation of individual decision: they oppose regulation of the content of political speech, even when such regulation might secure greater social order, and they oppose regulation of sexual literature and conduct even when such regulation has considerable majoritarian support. They are suspicious of the criminal law and anxious to reduce the extension of its provisions to behavior whose morality is controversial, and they support procedural constraints and devices, like rules against the admissibility of confessions, that makes it more difficult to secure criminal convictions.

I do not mean that everyone who holds any of these positions will or did hold them all. Some people who call themselves liberal do not support several elements of this package; some who call themselves conservative support most of them. But these are the positions that we use as a touchstone when we ask how liberal or conservative someone is; and indeed on which we now rely when we say that the line between liberals and conservatives is more blurred than once it was. I have omitted those positions that are only debatably elements of the liberal package, like support for military intervention in Vietnam, or the present campaign in support of human rights in Communist countries, or concern for more local participation in government or for consumer protection against manufacturers, or for the environment. I have also omitted debatable extension of liberal doctrines, like busing and quotas that discriminate in favor of minorities in education and employment. I shall assume that the positions that are uncontroversially liberal positions are the core of the liberal settlement. If my claim is right, that a particular conception of equality can be shown to be constitutive for that core of positions, we shall have, in that conception, a device for stating and testing the claim that some debatable position is also 'really' liberal.

II

Is there a thread of principle that runs through the core liberal positions, and that distinguishes these from the corresponding conservative positions? There is a familiar answer to this question that is mistaken, but mistaken in an illuminating way. The politics of democracies, according to this answer, recognizes several independent constitutive political ideals, the most important of which are the ideals of liberty and equality. Unfortunately, liberty and equality often conflict: sometimes the only effective means to promote equality require some limitation of liberty, and sometimes the consequences of promoting liberty are detrimental to equality. In these cases, good government consists in the best compromise between the competing ideals, but different politicians and citizens will make that compromise differently. Liberals tend relatively to favor equality more and liberty less than conservatives do, and the core set of liberal positions I described is the result of striking the balance that way.

This account offers a theory about what liberalism is. Liberalism shares the same constitutive principles with many other political theories, including conservatism, but is distinguished from these by attaching different relative importance to different principles. The theory therefore leaves room, on the spectrum it describes, for the radical who cares even more for equality and less for liberty than the liberal, and therefore stands even further away from the extreme conservative. The liberal becomes the man in the middle, which explains why liberalism is so often now considered wish-washy, an untenable compromise between two more forthright positions.

No doubt this description of American politics could be made more sophisticated. It might make room for other independent constitutive ideals shared by liberalism and its opponents, like stability or security, so that the compromises involved in particular decisions are made out to be more complex. But if the nerve of the theory remains the competition between liberty and equality as constitutive ideals, then the theory cannot succeed. In the first place, it does not satisfy condition (b) in the catalogue of conditions I set out. It seems to apply, at best, to only a limited number of the political controversies it tries to explain. It is designed for economic controversies, but is either irrelevant or misleading in the case of censorship and pornography, and indeed, in the criminal law generally.

But there is a much more important defect in this explanation. It assumes that liberty is measurable so that, if two political decisions each invades the liberty of a citizen, we can sensibly say that one decision takes more liberty away from him than the other. That assumption is necessary, because otherwise the postulate, that liberty is a constitutive ideal of both the liberal and conservative political structures, cannot be maintained. Even firm conservatives are content that their liberty to drive as they wish (for example to drive uptown on Lexington Avenue) may be invaded for the sake, not of some important competing political ideal, but only for marginal gains in convenience or orderly traffic patterns. But since traffic regulation plainly involves some loss of liberty, the conservative cannot be said to value liberty as such unless he is able to show that, for some reason, less liberty is lost by traffic regulation than by restrictions on, for example, free speech, or the liberty to sell for prices others are willing to pay, or whatever other liberty he takes to be fundamental.

But that is precisely what he cannot show, because we do not have a concept of liberty that is quantifiable in the way that demonstration would require. He cannot say, for example, that traffic regulations interfere less with what most men and women want to do than would a law forbidding them to speak out in favor of Communism, or a law requiring them not to fix their prices as they think best. Most people care more about driving than speaking for Communism, and have no occasion to fix prices even if they want to. I do not mean that we can make no sense of the idea of fundamental liberties, like freedom of speech. But we cannot argue in their favor by showing that they protect more liberty, taken to be an even roughly measurable commodity, than does the right to drive as we wish; the fundamental liberties are important because we value something else that they protect. But if that is so, then we cannot explain the difference between liberal and conservative political positions by supposing that the latter protect the commodity of liberty, valued for its own sake, more effectively than the former.[2]

It might now be said, however, that the other half of the liberty–equality explanation may be salvaged. Even if we cannot say that conservatives value liberty, as such, more than liberals, we can still say that they value equality less, and that the different political positions may be explained in that way. Conservatives tend to discount the importance of equality when set beside other goals, like general prosperity or even security; while liberals, in contrast, value equality relatively more, and radicals more still. Once again, it is apparent that this explanation is tailored to the economic controversies, and fits poorly with the non-economic controversies. Once again, however, its defects are more general and more important. We must identify more clearly the sense in which equality could be a constitutive ideal for either liberals or conservatives. Once we do so we shall see that it is misleading to say that the conservative values equality, in that sense, less than the liberal. We shall want to say, instead, that he has a different conception of what equality requires.

We must distinguish between two different principles that take equality to be a political ideal.[3] The first requires that the government treat all those in its charge *as equals*, that is, as entitled to its equal concern and respect. That is not an empty requirement: most of us do not suppose that we must, as individuals, treat our neighbor's children with the same concern as our own, or treat everyone we meet with the same respect. It is nevertheless plausible to think that any government should treat all its citizens as equals in that way. The second principle requires that the government treat all those in its charge *equally* in the distribution of some resource of opportunity, or at least work to secure the state of affairs in which they all are equal or more nearly equal in that respect. It is, of course, conceded by everyone that the government cannot make everyone equal in every respect, but people do disagree about how far government should try to secure equality in some particular resource; for example, in monetary wealth.

If we look only at the economic-political controversies, then we

[2] See Dworkin, *Taking Rights Seriously*, Chapter 12.
[3] See *Taking Rights Seriously*, pp. 227.

might well be justified in saying that liberals want more equality in the sense of the second principle than conservatives do. But it would be a mistake to conclude that they value equality in the sense of the first and more fundamental principle any more highly. I say that the first principle is more fundamental because I assume that, for both liberals and conservatives, the first is constitutive and the second derivative. Sometimes treating people equally is the only way to treat them as equals; but sometimes not. Suppose a limited amount of emergency relief is available for two equally populous areas injured by floods; treating the citizens of both areas as equals requires giving more aid to the more seriously devastated area rather than splitting the available funds equally. The conservative believes that in many other, less apparent, cases treating citizens equally amounts to not treating them as equals. He might concede, for example, that positive discrimination in university admissions will work to make the two races more nearly equal in wealth, but nevertheless maintain that such programs do not treat black and white university applicants as equals. If he is a utilitarian he will have a similar, though much more general, argument against any redistribution of wealth that reduces economic efficiency. He will say that the only way to treat people as equals is to maximize the average welfare of all members of community, counting gains and losses to all in the same scales, and that a free market is the only, or best, instrument for achieving that goal. This is not (I think) a good argument, but if the conservative who makes it is sincere he cannot be said to have discounted the importance of treating all citizens as equals.

So we must reject the simple idea that liberalism consists in a distinctive weighting between constitutive principles of equality and liberty. But our discussion of the idea of equality suggests a more fruitful line. I assume (as I said) that there is broad agreement within modern politics that the government must treat all its citizens with equal concern and respect. I do not mean to deny the great power of prejudice in, for example, American politics. But few citizens, and even fewer politicians, would now admit to political convictions that contradict the abstract principle of equal concern and respect. Different people hold, however, as our discussion made plain, very different conceptions of what that abstract principle requires in particular cases.

III

What does it mean for the government to treat its citizens as equals? That is, I think, the same question as the question of what it means for the government to treat all its citizens as free, or as independent, or with equal dignity. In any case, it is a question that has been central to political theory at least since Kant.

It may be answered in two fundamentally different ways. The first supposes that government must be neutral on what might be called the question of the good life. The second supposes that government cannot be neutral on that question, because it cannot treat its citizens as equal human beings without a theory of what human beings ought to be. I must explain that distinction further. Each person follows a more-or-less articulate conception of what gives value to life. The scholar who values a life of contemplation has such a conception; so does the television-watching, beer-drinking citizen who is fond of saying 'This is the life', though of course he has thought less about the issue and is less able to describe or defend his conception.

The first theory of equality supposes that political decisions must be, so far as is possible, independent of any particular conception of the good life, or of what gives value to life. Since the citizens of a society differ in their conceptions, the government does not treat them as equals if it prefers one conception to another, either because the officials believe that one is intrinsically superior, or because one is held by the more numerous or more powerful group. The second theory argues, on the contrary, that the content of equal treatment cannot be independent of some theory about the good for man or the good of life, because treating a person as an equal means treating him the way the good or truly wise person would wish to be treated. Good government consists in fostering or at least recognizing good lives; treatment as an equal consists in treating each person as if he were desirous of leading the life that is in fact good, at least so far as this is possible.

This distinction is very abstract, but it is also very important. I shall now argue that liberalism takes, as its constitutive political morality, the first conception of equality. I shall try to support that claim in this way. In the next section of this essay I shall show how it is plausible, and even likely, that a thoughtful person who accepted the first conception of equality would, given the economic and political circumstances of America in the last several decades, reach the positions I identified as the familiar core of liberal positions. If so, then the hypothesis satisfies the second of the conditions I described for a successful theory. In the following section I shall try to satisfy the third condition by showing how it is plausible and even likely that someone who held a particular version of the second theory of equality would reach what are normally regarded as the core of American conservative positions. I say 'a particular version of' because American conservatism does not follow automatically from rejecting the liberal theory of equality. The second (or non-liberal) theory of equality holds merely that the treatment government owes citizens is at least partly determined by some conception of the good life. Many political theories share that thesis, including theories as far apart as, for example, American conservatism and various forms of socialism or Marxism, though these will of course differ in the conception of the good life they adopt, and hence in the political institutions and decisions they endorse. In this respect, liberalism is decidedly not some compromise or half-way house between more forceful positions, but stands on one side of an important line that distinguishes it from all competitors taken as a group.

I shall not provide arguments in this essay that my theory of liberalism meets the first condition I described – that the theory must provide a political morality that it makes sense to suppose people in our culture hold – though I think it plain that the theory does meet this condition. The fourth condition requires that a theory be as abstract and general as the first three conditions allow. I doubt there will be objections to my theory on that account.

IV

I now define a liberal as someone who holds the first, or liberal, theory of what equality requires. Suppose that a liberal is asked to found a new state. He is required to dictate its constitution and fundamental institutions. He must propose a general theory of political distribution, that is, a theory of how whatever the community has to assign, by way of goods or resources or opportunities, should be assigned. He will arrive initially at something like this principle of rough equality: resources and opportunities should be distributed, so far as possible, equally, so that roughly the same share of whatever is available is devoted to satisfying the ambitions of each. Any other general aim of distribution will assume either that the fate of some people should be of greater concern than that of others, or that the ambitions or talents of some are more worthy, and should be supported more generously on that account.

Someone may object that this principle of rough equality is unfair because it ignores the fact that people have different tastes, and that some of these are more expensive to satisfy than others, so that, for example, the man who prefers champagne will need more funds if he is not to be frustrated than the man satisfied with beer. But the liberal may reply that tastes as to which people differ are, by and large, not afflictions, like diseases, but are rather cultivated, in accordance with each person's theory of what his life should be like.[4] The most effective neutrality, therefore, requires that the same share be devoted to each, so that the choice between expensive and less expensive tastes can be made by each person for himself, with no sense that his overall share will be enlarged by choosing a more expensive life, or that, whatever he chooses, his choice will subsidize those who have chosen more expensively.[5]

But what does the principle of rough equality of distribution require in practice? If all resources were distributed directly by the government through grants of food, housing, and so forth; if every opportunity citizens have were provided directly by the government through the provisions of civil and criminal law; if every citizen had exactly the same talents; if every citizen started his life with no more than what any other citizen had at the start; and if every citizen had exactly the same theory of the good life and hence exactly the same scheme of preferences as every other citizen, including preferences between productive activity of dif-

---

[4] See Scanlon, 'Preference and Urgency', *J. Phil.*, LXXII, 655.

[5] A very different objection calls attention to the fact that some people are afflicted with incapacities like blindness or mental disease, so that they require more resources to satisfy the *same* scheme of preferences. That is a more appealing objection to my principle of rough equality of treatment, but it calls, not for choosing a different basic principle of distribution, but for corrections in the application of the principle like those I consider later.

ferent forms and leisure, then the principle of rough equality of treatment could be satisfied simply by equal distributions of everything to be distributed and by civil and criminal laws of universal application. Government would arrange for production that maximized the mix of goods, including jobs and leisure, that everyone favored, distributing the product equally.

Of course, none of these conditions of similarity holds. But the moral relevance of different sorts of diversity are very different, as may be shown by the following exercise. Suppose all the conditions of similarity I mentioned did hold except the last: citizens have different theories of the good and hence different preferences. They therefore disagree about what product the raw materials and labor and savings of the community should be used to produce, and about which activities should be prohibited or regulated so as to make others possible or easier. The liberal, as lawgiver, now needs mechanisms to satisfy the principles of equal treatment in spite of these disagreements. He will decide that there are no better mechanisms available, as general political institutions, than the two main institutions of our own political economy: the economic market, for decisions about what goods shall be produced and how they shall be distributed, and representative democracy, for collective decisions about what conduct shall be prohibited or regulated so that other conduct might be made possible or convenient. Each of these familiar institutions may be expected to provide a more egalitarian division than any other general arrangement. The market, if it can be made to function efficiently, will determine for each product a price that reflects the cost in resources of material, labor and capital that might have been applied to produce something different that someone else wants. That cost determines, for anyone who consumes that product, how much his account should be charged in computing the egalitarian division of social resources. It provides a measure of how much more his account should be charged for a house than a book, and for one book rather than another. The market will also provide, for the laborer, a measure of how much should be credited to his account for his choice of productive activity over leisure, and for one activity rather than another. It will tell us, through the price it puts on his labor, how much he should gain or lose by his decision to pursue one career rather than another.

These measurements make a citizen's own distribution a function of the personal preferences of others as well as of his own, and it is the sum of these personal preferences that fixes the true cost to the community of meeting his own preferences for goods and activities. The egalitarian distribution, which requires that the cost of satisfying one person's preferences should as far as is possible be equal to the cost of satisfying another's, cannot be enforced unless those measurements are made.

We are familiar with the anti-egalitarian consequences of free enterprise in practice; it may therefore seem paradoxical that the liberal as lawgiver should choose a market economy for reasons of equality rather than efficiency. But, under the special condition that people differ only in preferences for goods and activities, the market is more egalitarian than any alternative of comparable generality. The most plausible alternative would be to allow decisions of production, investment, price and wage to be made by elected officials in a socialist economy. But what principles should officials use in making those decisions? The liberal might tell them to mimic the decisions that a market would make if it was working efficiently under proper competition and full knowledge. This mimicry would be, in practice, much less efficient than an actual market would be. In any case, unless the liberal had reason to think it would be much more efficient, he would have good reason to reject it. Any minimally efficient mimicking of a hypothetical market would require invasions of privacy to determine what decisions individuals would make if forced actually to pay for their investment, consumption and employment decisions at market rates, and this information gathering would be, in many other ways, much more expensive than an actual market. Inevitably, moreover, the assumptions officials make about how people would behave in a hypothetical market reflect the officials' own beliefs about how people should behave. So there would be, for the liberal, little to gain and much to lose in a socialist economy in which officials were asked to mimic a hypothetical market.

But any other instructions would be a direct violation of the liberal theory of what equality requires, because if a decision is made to produce and sell goods at a price below the price a market would fix, then those who prefer those goods are, *pro tanto*, receiving more than an equal share of the resources of the community at the expense of those who would prefer some other use of the resources. Suppose the limited demand for books, matched against the demand for competing uses for wood-pulp, would fix the price of books at a point higher than the socialist managers of the economy will charge; those who want books are having less charged to their account than the egalitarian principle would require. It might be said that in a socialist economy books are simply valued more, because they are inherently more worthy uses of social resources, quite apart from the popular demand for books. But the liberal theory of equality rules out that appeal to the inherent value of one theory of what is good in life.

In a society in which people differed only in preferences, then, a market would be favored for its egalitarian consequences. Inequality of monetary wealth would be the consequence only of the fact that some preferences are more expensive than others, including the preference for leisure time rather than the most lucrative productive activity. But we must now return to the real world. In the actual society for which the liberal must construct political institutions, there are all the other differences. Talents are not distributed equally, so the decision of one person to work in a factory rather than a law firm, or not to work at all, will be governed in large part by his abilities rather than his preferences for work or between work and leisure. The institutions of wealth, which allow people to dispose of what they receive by gift, mean that children of the successful will start with more wealth than the children of the unsuccessful. Some people have special needs, because they are handicapped; their handicap will not only disable them from the most productive and lucrative employment, but will incapacitate them from using the proceeds of whatever employment they find as efficiently, so that they will need more than those who are not handicapped to satisfy identical ambitions.

These inequalities will have great, often catastrophic, effects on the distribution that a market economy will provide. But, unlike differences in preferences, the differences these inequalities make are indefensible according to the liberal conception of equality. It is obviously obnoxious to the liberal conception, for example, that someone should have more of what the community as a whole has to distribute because he or his father had superior skill or luck.

The liberal lawgiver therefore faces a difficult task. His conception of equality requires an economic system that produces certain inequalities (those that reflect the true differential costs of goods and opportunities) but not others (those that follow from differences in ability, inheritance, etc.). The market produces both the required and the forbidden inequalities, and there is no alternative system that can be relied upon to produce the former without the latter.

The liberal must be tempted, therefore, to a reform of the market through a scheme of redistribution that leaves its pricing system relatively intact but sharply limits, at least, the inequalities in welfare that his initial principle prohibits. No solution will seem perfect. The liberal may find the best answer in a scheme of welfare rights financed through redistributive income and inheritance taxes of the conventional sort, which redistributes just to the Rawlsian point, that is, to the point at which the worst-off group would be harmed rather than benefited by further transfers. In that case, he will remain a reluctant capitalist, believing that a market economy so reformed is superior, from the standpoint of his conception of equality, to any practical socialist alternative. Or he may believe that the redistribution that is possible in a capitalist economy will be so inadequate, or will be purchased at the cost of such inefficiency, that it is better to proceed in a more radical way, by substituting socialist for market decisions over a large part of the economy, and then relying on the political process to insure that prices are set in a manner at least roughly consistent with his conception of equality. In that case he will be a reluctant socialist, who acknowledges the egalitarian defects of socialism but counts them as less severe than the practical alternatives. In either case, he chooses a mixed economic system – either redistributive capitalism or limited socialism – not in order to compromise antagonistic ideals of efficiency and equality, but to achieve the best practical realization of the demands of equality itself.

Let us assume that in this manner the liberal either refines or partially retracts his original selection of a market economy. He must now consider the second of the two familiar institutions he first selected, which is representative democracy. Democracy is justified because it enforces the right of each person to respect and concern as an individual; but in practice the decisions of a democratic majority may often violate that right, according to the liberal theory of what the right requires. Suppose a legislature elected by a majority decides to make criminal some act (like speaking in favor of an unpopular political position, or participating in eccentric sexual practices) not because the act deprives others of opportunities they want, but because the majority disapproves of those views or that sexual morality. The political decision, in other words, reflects not simply some accommodation of the *personal* preferences of everyone, in such a way as to make the opportunities of all as nearly equal as may be, but the domination of one set of *external* preferences, that is, preferences people have about what others shall do or have.[6] The decision invades rather than enforces the right of citizens to be treated as equals.

How can the liberal protect citizens against that sort of violation of their fundamental right? It will not do for the liberal simply to instruct legislators, in some constitutional exhortation, to disregard the external preferences of their constituents. Citizens will vote these preferences in electing their representatives, and a legislator who chooses to ignore them will not survive. In any case, it is sometimes impossible to distinguish, even by introspection, the external and personal components of a political position: this is the case, for example, with associational preferences, which are the preferences some people have for opportunities, like the opportunity to attend public schools, but only with others of the same 'background'.

The liberal, therefore, needs a scheme of civil rights, whose effect will be to determine those political decisions that are antecedently likely to reflect strong external preferences, and to remove those decisions from majoritarian political institutions altogether. Of course, the scheme of rights necessary to do this will depend on general facts about the prejudices and other external preferences of the majority at any given time, and different liberals will disagree about what is needed at any particular time.[7] But the rights encoded in the Bill of Rights of the United States Constitution, as interpreted (on the whole) by the Supreme Court, are

---

[6] *Taking Rights Seriously*, pp. 234ff, 275.

[7] See Dworkin, 'Social Sciences and Constitutional Rights', *The Educational Forum*, XLI (March 1977), 271.

those that a substantial number of liberals would think reasonably well suited to what the United States now requires (though most would think that the protection of the individual in certain important areas, including sexual publication and practice, are much too weak).

The main parts of the criminal law, however, present a special problem not easily met by a scheme of civil rights that disable the legislature from taking certain political decisions. The liberal knows that many of the most important decisions required by an effective criminal law are not made by legislators at all, but by prosecutors deciding whom to prosecute for what crime, and by juries and judges deciding whom to convict and what sentences to impose. He also knows that these decisions are antecedently very likely to be corrupted by the external preferences of those who make these decisions because those they judge, typically, have attitudes and ways of life very different from their own. The liberal does not have available, as protection against these decisions, any strategy comparable to the strategy of civil rights that simply remove a decision from an institution. Decisions to prosecute, convict and sentence must be made by someone. But he has available, in the notion of procedural rights, a different device to protect equality in a different way. He will insist that criminal procedure be structured to achieve a margin of safety in decisions, so that the process is biased strongly against the conviction of the innocent. It would be a mistake to suppose that the liberal thinks that these procedural rights will improve the *accuracy* of the criminal process, that is, the probability that any particular decision about guilt or innocence will be the right one. Procedural rights intervene in the process, even at the cost of inaccuracy, to compensate in a rough way for the antecedent risk that a criminal process, especially if it is largely administered by one class against another, will be corrupted by the impact of external preferences that cannot be eliminated directly. This is, of course, only the briefest sketch of how various substantive and procedural civil rights follow from the liberal's initial conception of equality; it is meant to suggest, rather than demonstrate, the more precise argument that would be available for more particular rights.

So the liberal, drawn to the economic market and to political

democracy for distinctly egalitarian reasons, finds that these
institutions will produce inegalitarian results unless he adds to
his scheme different sorts of individual rights. These rights will
function as trump cards held by individuals; they will enable
individuals to resist particular decisions in spite of the fact that
these decisions are or would be reached through the normal workings of general institutions that are not themselves challenged.
The ultimate justification for these rights is that they are necessary
to protect equal concern and respect; but they are not to be
understood as representing equality in contrast to some other goal
or principle served by democracy or the economic market. The
familiar idea, for example, that rights of restribution are justified
by an ideal of equality that overrides the efficiency ideals of the
market in certain cases, has no place in liberal theory. For the
liberal, rights are justified, not by some principle in competition
with an independent justification of the political and economic
institutions they qualify, but in order to make more perfect the
only justification on which these other institutions may themselves
rely. If the liberal arguments for a particular right are sound, then
the right is an unqualified improvement in political morality, not
a necessary but regrettable compromise of some other independent
goal, like economic efficiency.

V

I said that the conservative holds one among a number of possible
alternatives to the liberal conception of equality. Each of these
alternatives shares the opinion that treating a person with respect
requires treating him as the good man would wish to be treated.
The conservative supposes that the good man would wish to be
treated in accordance with the principles of a special sort of
society, which I shall call the virtuous society. A virtuous society
has these general features. Its members share a sound conception
of virtue, that is, of the qualities and dispositions people should
strive to have and exhibit. They share this conception of virtue
not only privately, as individuals, but publicly: they believe their
community, in its social and political activity, exhibits virtues, and
that they have a responsibility, as citizens, to promote these

virtues. In that sense they treat the lives of other members of their community as part of their own lives. The conservative position is not the only position that relies on this ideal of the virtuous society (some forms of socialism rely on it as well). But the conservative is distinct in believing that his own society, with its present institutions, is a virtuous society for the special reason that its history and common experience are better guides to sound virtue than any non-historical and therefore abstract deduction of virtue from first principles could provide.

Suppose a conservative is asked to draft a constitution for a society generally like ours, which he believes to be virtuous. Like the liberal, he will see great merit in the familiar institutions of political democracy and an economic market. The appeal of these institutions will be very different for the conservative, however. The economic market, in practice, assigns greater rewards to those who, because they have the virtues of talent and industry, supply more of what is wanted by the other members of the virtuous society; and that is, for the conservative, the paradigm of fairness in distribution. Political democracy distributes opportunities, through the provisions of the civil and criminal law, as the citizens of a virtuous society wish it to be distributed, and that process will provide more scope for virtuous activity and less for vice than any less democratic technique. Democracy has a further advantage, moreover, that no other technique could have. It allows the community to use the processes of legislation to reaffirm, as a community, its public conception of virtue.

The appeal of the familiar institutions to the conservative is, therefore, very different from their appeal to the liberal. Since the conservative and the liberal both find the familiar institutions useful, though for different reasons, the existence of these institutions, as institutions, will not necessarily be a point of controversy between them. But they will disagree sharply over which corrective devices, in the form of individual rights, are necessary in order to maintain justice, and the disagreement will not be a matter of degree. The liberal, as I said, finds the market defective principally because it allows morally irrelevant differences, like differences in talent, to affect distribution, and he therefore considers that those who have less talent, as the market judges talent, have a right to some form of redistribution in the name of justice.

But the conservative prizes just the feature of the market that puts a premium on talents prized in the community, because these are, in a virtuous community, virtues. So he will find no genuine merit, but only expediency, in the idea of redistribution. He will allow room, of course, for the virtue of charity, for it is a virtue that is part of the public catalogue; but he will prefer private charity to public, because it is a purer expression of that virtue. He may accept public charity as well, particularly when it seems necessary to retain the political allegiance of those who would otherwise suffer too much to tolerate a capitalist society at all. But public charity, justified either on grounds of virtue or expediency, will seem to the conservative a compromise with the primary justification of the market, rather than, as redistribution seems to the liberal, an improvement in that primary justification.

Nor will the conservative find the same defects in representative democracy that the liberal finds there. The conservative will not aim to exclude moralistic or other external preferences from the democratic process by any scheme of civil rights; on the contrary, it is the pride of democracy, for him, that external preferences are legislated into a public morality. But the conservative will find different defects in democracy, and he will contemplate a different scheme of rights to diminish the injustice they work.

The economic market distributes rewards for talents valued in the virtuous society, but since these talents are unequally distributed, wealth will be concentrated, and the wealthy will be at the mercy of an envious political majority anxious to take by law what it cannot take by talent. Justice requires some protection for the successful. The conservative will be (as historically he has been) anxious to hold some line against extensions of the vote to those groups most likely to be envious, but there is an apparent conflict between the ideals of abstract equality, even in the conservative conception, and disenfranchisement of large parts of the population. In any case, if conservatism is to be politically powerful, it must not threaten to exclude from political power those who would be asked to consent, formally or tacitly, to their own exclusion. The conservative will find more appeal in the different, and politically much more feasible, idea of rights to property.

These rights have the same force, though of course radically different content, as the liberal's civil rights. The liberal will, for his own purposes, accept some right to property, because he will count some sovereignty over a range of personal possessions essential to dignity. But the conservative will strive for rights to property of a very different order; he will want rights that protect, not some minimum dominion over a range of possessions independently shown to be desirable, but an unlimited dominion over whatever has been acquired through an institution that defines and rewards talent.

The conservative will not, of course, follow the liberal in the latter's concern for procedural rights in the criminal process. He will accept the basic institutions of criminal legislation and trial as proper; but he will see, in the possible acquittal of the guilty, not simply an inefficiency in the strategy of deterrence, but an affront to the basic principle that the censure of vice is indispensable to the honor of virtue. He will believe, therefore, that just criminal procedures are those that improve the antecedent probability that particular decisions of guilt or innocence will be accurate. He will support rights against interrogation or self-incrimination, for example, when such rights seem necessary to protect against torture or other means likely to elicit a confession from the innocent; but he will lose his concern for such rights when non-coercion can be guaranteed in other ways.

The fair-minded conservative will be concerned about racial discrimination, but his concern will differ from the concern of the liberal, and the remedies he will countenance will also be different. The distinction between equality of opportunity and equality of result is crucial to the conservative: the institutions of the economic market and representative democracy cannot achieve what he supposes they do unless each citizen has an equal opportunity to capitalize on his genuine talents and other virtues in the contest these institutions provide. But since the conservative knows that these virtues are unequally distributed, he also knows that equality of opportunity must have been denied if the outcome of the contest is equality of result.

The fair conservative must, therefore, attend to the charge that prejudice denies equality of opportunity between members of different races, and he must accept the justice of remedies designed to reinstate that equality, so far as this may be possible. But he will steadily oppose any form of 'affirmative action' that offers special opportunities, like places in medical school or jobs, on criteria other than some proper conception of the virtue appropriate to the reward.

The issue of gun control, which I have thus far not mentioned, is an excellent illustration of the power of the conservative's constitutive political morality. He favors strict control of sexual publication and practice, but he opposes parallel control of the ownership or use of guns, though of course guns are more dangerous than sex. President Ford, in the second Carter–Ford debate, put the conservative position of gun control especially clearly. Sensible conservatives do not dispute that private and uncontrolled ownership of guns leads to violence, because it puts guns in circulation that bad men may use badly. But (President Ford said) if we meet that problem by not allowing good men to have guns, we are punishing the wrong people. It is, of course, distinctive to the conservative's position to regard regulation as condemnation and hence as punishment. But he must regard regulation that way, because he believes that opportunities should be distributed, in a virtuous society, so as to promote virtuous acts at the expense of vicious ones.

VI

In place of a conclusion, I shall say something, though not much, about two of the many important questions raised by what I have said. The first is the question posed in the first section of the essay. Does the theory of liberalism I described answer the sceptical thesis? Does it explain our present uncertainty about what liberalism now requires, and whether it is a genuine and tenable political theory? A great part of that uncertainty can be traced, as I said, to doubts about the connections between liberalism and the suddenly unfashionable idea of economic growth. The opinion is popular that some form of utilitarianism, which does take growth to be a value in itself, is constitutive of liberalism; but my arguments, if successful, show that this opinion is a mistake. Economic growth, as conventionally measured, was a derivative element in New Deal liberalism. It seemed to play a useful role in achieving the complex egalitarian distribution of resources that liberalism requires. If it now appears that economic growth injures more than it aids the liberal conception of equality, then the liberal is free to reject or curtail growth as a strategy. If the effect of growth is debatable, as I believe it is, then liberals will be uncertain, and appear to straddle the issue.

But the matter is more complicated than that analysis makes it seem, because economic growth may be deplored for many different reasons, some of which are plainly not available to the liberal. There is a powerful sentiment that a simpler way of life is better, in itself, than the life of consumption most Americans have recently preferred; this simpler life requires living in harmony with nature, and is therefore disturbed when, for example, a beautiful mountainside is spoiled by strip mining for the coal that lies within it. Should the mountainside be saved, in order to protect a way of life that depends upon it, either by regulation that prohibits mining, or by acquisition with taxpayers' money of a national park? May a liberal support such policies, consistently with his constitutive political morality? If he believes that government intervention is necessary to achieve a fair distribution of resources, on the ground that the market does not fairly reflect the preferences of those who want a park against those who want what the coal will produce, then he has a standard, egalitarian reason for supporting intervention. But suppose he does not believe that, but rather believes that those who want the park have a superior conception of what a truly worthwhile life is. A non-liberal may support conservation on that theory; but a liberal may not.

Suppose, however, that the liberal holds a different, more complex, belief about the importance of preserving natural resources. He believes that the conquest of unspoilt terrain by the consumer economy is self-fueling and irreversible, and that this process will make a way of life that has been desired and found satisfying in the past unavailable to future generations, and indeed to the future of those who now seem unaware of its appeal. He fears that this way of life will become unknown, so that the process is not neutral amongst competing ideas of the good life, but in fact destructive of the very possibility of some of these. In that case the liberal has reasons for a program of conservation that are not only consistent with his constitutive morality, but in fact sponsored by it.

I raise these possible lines of argument, not to provide the liberal with an easier path to a popular political position, but to illustrate the complexity of the issues that the new politics has provided. Liberalism seems precise and powerful when it is relatively clear what practical political positions are derivative from its fundamental constitutive morality; on these occasions politics allows what I called a liberal settlement of political positions. But such a settlement is fragile, and when it dissolves liberals must regroup, first through study and analysis, which will encourage a fresh and deeper understanding of what liberalism is, and then through the formation of a new and contemporary program for liberals. The study and theory are not yet in progress, and the new program is not yet in sight.

The second question I wish to mention, finally, is a question I have not touched at all. What is to be said in favor of liberalism? I do not suppose that I have made liberalism more attractive by arguing that its constitutive morality is a theory of equality that requires official neutrality amongst theories of what is valuable in life. That argument will provoke a variety of objections. It might be said that liberalism so conceived rests on scepticism about theories of the good, or that it is based on a mean view of human nature that assumes that human beings are atoms who can exist and find self-fulfillment apart from political community, or that it is self-contradictory because liberalism must itself be a theory of the good, or that it denies to political society its highest function and ultimate justification, which is that society must help its members to achieve what is in fact good. The first three of these objections need not concern us for long, because they are based on philosophical mistakes which I can quickly name if not refute. Liberalism cannot be based on scepticism. Its constitutive morality provides that human beings must be treated as equals by their government, not because there is no right and wrong in political morality, but because that is what is right. Liberalism does not rest on any special theory of personality, nor does it deny that most human beings will think that what is good for them is that they be active in society. Liberalism is not self-contradictory: the liberal conception of equality is a principle of political organization that is required by justice, not a way of life for individuals, and liberals, as such, are indifferent as to whether people choose to speak out on political matters, or to lead eccentric lives, or otherwise to behave as liberals are supposed to prefer.

But the fourth objection cannot so easily be set aside. There is no easy way to demonstrate the proper role of institutions that have a monopoly of power over the lives of others; reasonable and moral men will disagree. The issue is at bottom the issue I identified: what is the content of the respect that is necessary to dignity and independence?

That raises problems in moral philosophy and in the philosophy of mind that are fundamental for political theory though not discussed here; but this essay does bear on one issue sometimes thought to be relevant. It is sometimes said that liberalism must be wrong because it assumes that the opinions people have about the sort of lives they want are self-generated, whereas these opinions are in fact the products of the economic system or other aspects of the society in which they live. That would be an objection to liberalism if liberalism were based on some form of preference-utilitarianism which argued that justice in distribution consists in maximizing the extent to which people have what they happen to want. It is useful to point out, against that preference-utilitarianism, that since the preferences people have are formed by the system of distribution already in place, these preferences will tend to support that system, which is both circular and unfair. But liberalism, as I have described it, does not make the content of preferences the test of fairness in distribution. On the contrary, it is anxious to protect individuals whose needs are special or whose ambitions are eccentric from the fact that more popular preferences are institutionally and socially reinforced, for that is the effect and justification of the liberal's scheme of economic and political rights. Liberalism responds to the claim, that preferences are caused by systems of distribution, with the sensible answer that in that case it is all the more important that distribution be fair in itself, not as tested by the preferences it produces.